Becoming A Counselor

SAMUEL T. GLADDING

5999 Stevenson Avenue
Alexandria, VA 22304
www.counseling.org

Becoming A Counselor

The Light, the Bright, and the Serious

10 9 8 7 6 5 4 3 2 1

American Counseling Association
5999 Stevenson Avenue
Alexandria, VA 22304

Director of Publications
Carolyn C. Baker

Production Manager
Bonny Gaston

Copy Editor
Sharon Doyle

Cover design by Martha Woolsey

Library of Congress Cataloging-in-Publication Data

Gladding, Samuel T.
Becoming a counselor: the light, the bright, and the serious/by Samuel T. Gladding
p. cm.
Includes bibliographical references.
ISBN 1-55620-191-5 (alk. paper)
1. Counseling. 2. Counselors. I. Title.

BF637.C6 G525 2001
158'.3—dc21 2001040178

Dedication

TO THOMAS J. SWEENEY

An active and strong voice for counseling as a profession,
the founder of Chi Sigma Iota (counseling academic and
professional honor society international),
a friend and mentor.

Table of Contents

Section | four

SKILLS AND PROCESSES

Section | five

MULTICULTURAL AND SPIRITUAL CONSIDERATIONS

Section | six

THE INFLUENCES OF COLLEAGUES, FRIENDS, AND FAMILY

Section | seven

WORKING WITH GROUPS AND FAMILIES

Section | eight

PROFESSIONAL DEVELOPMENT

Section | nine

DEVELOPMENTAL CONSIDERATIONS

Section | ten

TERMINATION

Preface

Some events change your life. Most are not so powerful. Critical occurrences that have an impact are landmark experiences such as leaving home, the death of a parent, the achievement of a goal, failure, an accident, a chance encounter, or a natural disaster. Other transitional times may be less notable but still influential, such as moments of insight, prejudice, or simple acts of kindness. Outside of these memorable incidents, the rest of our existence is rather mundane and routine. Thus, we may be at a loss to recall what we ate or to whom we talked two days ago because neither was significant in life-changing or life-giving ways.

In counseling we see people at crisis points. They are usually ready or willing to make necessary changes, some of which are dramatic. However, as clinicians we seldom remember most of the people we encounter because the helping process is more routine than revolutionary. My experiences reflect that pattern. I can recall only a few of the hundreds of individuals I have assisted. Yet, some events in my personal and professional life have been turning points that have influenced my growth and development in a manner similar to those situations that have most affected my clients. You have had (or most likely will have) some similar experiences. These times are filled with a plethora of emotions and thoughts as well as new behaviors.

The vignettes in this text are representative of many universal dimensions involved in becoming a counselor and helping professional. In these stories, you will find examples of

- the light, that is, the humorous aspects of life and counseling;
- the bright, that is, the insightful nature of life and counseling; and
- the serious, that is, the deeper and more sobering parts of life and counseling.

Sometimes these three dimensions occur simultaneously and are obvious. Sometimes they are sequential and subtle. Regardless, they are a part of the experience of both novice and veteran counselors.

Although the incidents in these stories are unique, they are also broad-based. You may find yourself identifying with them and their applicability to you. The "Points to Ponder" section at the conclusion of each chapter is an especially good place for such reflections. In any case, it is my hope that this book will assist you in living a richer, fuller, deeper, and more meaningful life through gaining insight into yourself and the processes involved in the bittersweet process of choice and change.

In reading this text, remember that some incidents represented here, mainly those that occurred in my own life, are true. However, most of the stories in this book are based on facts that have been altered or embellished. Thus, in all circumstances, characters who are a part of these episodes (unless specifically identified) have been disguised through multiple means such as being combined with similar people in a composite, having their names changed, having their genders switched, or having their presenting problem modified.

There are a number of people who have been pivotal in the publication of this book. Clients, colleagues, and situations are the key sources for what appears on these pages. However, the one who has done the most to transpose my reflections into readable prose is Anita Hughes, my assistant at Wake Forest University, who typed, organized, and edited this material in an exemplary manner. I could not have completed the task without her. My colleagues in the counselor education program at Wake Forest University, especially Donna Henderson, Debbie Newsome, Laura Veach, Tom Elmore, Pamela Karr, and John Anderson, have also been most supportive. I am likewise grateful for the positive input into my life by Thomas J. Sweeney, to whom this book is dedicated, and the encouragement and constructive comments of Carolyn Baker, Director of Publications at the American Counseling Association (ACA). My gratitude is also extended to the publication committee members of ACA who reviewed and favorably recommended this work. Finally, I am indebted to my wife, Claire, and our children, Ben, Nate, and Tim, for the rich memories they have provided me in regard to counseling and life. Becoming a counselor is a continuous and challenging process.

Samuel T. Gladding

About the Author

Samuel T. Gladding is professor of counselor education and director of the counselor education program at Wake Forest University in Winston-Salem, North Carolina. He has been a practicing counselor in both public and private agencies since 1971. His leadership in the field of counseling includes service as

- president of the Association for Counselor Education and Supervision (ACES),
- president of the Association for Specialists in Group Work (ASGW),
- president of Chi Sigma Iota (counseling academic and professional honor society international), and
- vice president of the Counseling Association for Humanistic Education and Development (C-AHEAD).

Gladding is the former editor of the *Journal for Specialists in Group Work* and the ASGW newsletter. He is also the author of more than 100 professional publications. In 1999, he was cited as being in the top 1% of contributors to the flagship journal of the American Counseling Association, the *Journal of Counseling & Development,* for the 15-year period from 1978 to 1993. Some of Gladding's most recent books are *The Counseling Dictionary* (2001), *Counseling: A Comprehensive Profession* (4th ed.) (2000), *Group Work: A Counseling Specialty* (3rd ed.) (1999), *Counseling as an Art: The Creative Arts in Counseling* (2nd ed.) (1998a), and *Family Therapy: History, Theory and Process* (3rd ed.) (2002).

Gladding's previous academic appointments have been at the University of Alabama at Birmingham, Fairfield University (Connecticut), and Rockingham Community College (Wentworth, North Carolina). He was also Director of Children's Services at the Rockingham County (North Carolina) Mental Health Center. Gladding received his degrees from Wake Forest University (BA, MA, Ed), Yale University (MAR), and the University of North Carolina at Greensboro (PhD). He is a National Certified Counselor (NCC), a Certified Clinical Mental Health Counselor (CCMHC), and a Licensed Professional Counselor (North Carolina). He is a former member of the Alabama Board of Examiners in Counseling.

Gladding is the recipient of numerous honors, including

- the Chi Sigma Iota Thomas J. Sweeney Professional Leadership Award,
- the Counseling Association for Humanistic Education and Development Joseph W. and Lucille U. Hollis Outstanding Publication Award,
- the Association for Counselor Education and Supervision Professional Leadership Award,
- the Association for Specialists in Group Work Eminent Career Award, and
- the North Carolina Counseling Association's Ella Stephen Barrett Award for leadership and service to the counseling profession.

Dr. Gladding is married to the former Claire Tillson and is the father of three children—Ben, Nate, and Tim. Outside of counseling, he enjoys tennis, swimming, and humor.

Section | one

INITIATION INTO THE PROFESSION

Templeman/Gladding travels in me
a restless presence, a history
of time and people who walked the world
long before my birth.
Attuned to the sound of their stories
I wince at their failures
and bask in their glories.
Knowing now I am on my own
I am aware I am never alone
for they are a part of my life.

We all begin our journey to be counselors as people who are seeking a purpose greater than ourselves and for the benefit of others. In the process, we often find a new awareness of who we are and what we can and should do. Our progress of becoming is a paradox at times. The more we let go of the roles that have confined us, the greater freedom we have. Our flexibility also increases. Yet, in this awareness, we realize that much of whom we are developing into is linked to what we have inherited in both our personal and professional histories. We are different from our ancestors, but their legacies assist us in learning the art of helping others and ourselves.

In the four vignettes in this section, I have highlighted some learning that took place early in my career. On a personal level, the stories are about discovery of both self and methods of assisting others. On a professional level, these brief snapshots are about growth and insight that not only are unique in these particular situations but also have universal qualities.

chapter | 1

THE CALLING

The sun was low in the sky as I hit the Washington, DC beltway. I was driving from New Haven, Connecticut, to Atlanta, Georgia, in a 1968 Mustang and was fighting fatigue and the glare off the windshield. Other cars were passing me by, and I wondered if life might not be doing the same unless I made an adjustment and shifted gears. I was a second-year student at Yale Divinity School, and through a self-assessment of my thoughts and feelings over the past few months, I had realized I was not going to be a divine, let alone a minister. Although that revelation may seem minor now, it was a major epiphany for me in the spring of 1970. I had had a plan for 21 years to follow in my maternal grandfather's footsteps. I had been named for him, grown up on Church Street, and been a member of a very religious family. The agenda was loaded. I always thought I would spend my Sunday mornings behind a pulpit (most likely standing on a Coca-Cola crate) but definitely not sitting in a pew or sleeping late. Now, reality had set in, and I was headed south both literally and figuratively.

Yet, as fate would have it that day, I did not make it all the way to my parents' home in Atlanta. Instead, I wound up spending the night in Winston-Salem, North Carolina, the city that was the home to my undergraduate alma mater, Wake Forest University. So the next morning, before completing my journey, I decided to visit the campus and the former Dean of Students, Dr. Tom Elmore, an administrator I had known and trusted for a number of years. Tom had recently resigned the Dean of Students position to start a counselor education program. After exchanging pleasantries, I told him of my struggles, and with his best attending skills, he listened. Then he said five words that changed my life.

"Why don't you try counseling?"

Not realizing that he meant that maybe I should seek personal counseling, I thought he was implying that I should enroll in a counseling program. Thus, the next fall, having finished Yale, I matriculated into the counseling program at Wake Forest. It was a move filled with the instant recognition that the profession would be my psychological home for life . . . and it has been.

chapter | 2

ENCOUNTERING THE UNEXPECTED: BANDITS

It was a hot summer afternoon in North Carolina. I was driving down rural roads to my first job in a mental health center following the morning of my graduation. With a master's of counseling degree in hand, I was sure that little stood between me and success other than the 50 miles from the city of Winston-Salem to the little town of Wentworth. Thus, on that June day I took in the scenery and daydreamed. However, my euphoria was disrupted by an unexpected event along the way. There before me, in hand-painted letters, were these words on a signpost: "Bandits—Straight Ahead."

"Holy Lone Ranger!" I said to myself. "Where am I going, and will I get there in one piece?" (My new employer had failed to tell me that I might encounter some mid-route turbulence on the way to work.)

Nevertheless, out of curiosity and in trepidation, I continued. As I drove I saw other equally crude but well-constructed signs informing me of the presence of bandits—15 miles, 10 miles, 5 miles, 1 mile, and finally "just around the corner." In a gallows humor I muttered anxiously to myself: "If it pays to advertise, these guys are going to make a killing." Thus, as I drove the last few hundred yards, I did so knowing I had been forewarned.

To my relief, however, what I encountered around that last bend in the road was not dangerous. Rather, it was a dilapidated wooden building, badly in need of repair, with a bundle of items piled out in front and a banner over the door that read: "Cheap! Cheap! Cheap! My brother steals and I sell it. Welcome to Bandits!"

While I passed up the opportunity to go view what was hot (and what was not), the memory of that day has stayed with me over the years. The reason, I think, is the impact and message of the road signs that I read. What they conveyed outwardly and what was displayed ultimately was a dichotomy. Similarly, when we meet with clients, we may receive initial signs that do not reveal the reality of their lives. On such occasions, the experiences we have turn out differently than anything we would ever have imagined on our way to work.

chapter | 3

"UH-HUH" IS NEVER ENOUGH

My initial education and credential as a counselor was a master's degree. I did my practicum/internship in the campus counseling center in a Rogerian, person-centered fashion. I said "uh-huh" long before Ray Charles and Pepsico ever thought it was the right thing to do in a commercial. Amazingly, my clients got better, and when I left the center I carried Rogerian techniques and great optimism with me to the rural mental health facility where I was initially employed. I was the "uh-huh counselor," and I was ready to heal the world. My expectations of becoming another Carl Rogers quickly and dramatically faded, however, the first week of my employment when I realized that "uh-huh" is never enough.

The case that awakened me came on the Friday of the first week of work. All during the week preceding that event, my main job had been to learn how to play cards with clients who were severely disturbed. Growing up in a strict Baptist home with a mother who was a PK (preacher's kid), I had never been allowed to possess playing cards, let alone play card games. I am sure the director of the mental health center thought that learning such games would be good for me and the clients who came to the center to play on a regular basis. At first it was fun, but I grew restless as the week wore on.

I was tired of dealing (and losing) and anxious to see real neurotic people who I thought needed my services. Sure enough, at 4:59 p.m. on the first Friday of my career, a call came to the center from a social service agency that was requesting help in an emergency. I was standing by the secretary when the call came in, awkwardly shuffling cards in my hands out of a sense of boredom while simultaneously shuffling my feet slowly in anticipation of an opportunity. As the conversation dragged on, I shuffled my feet faster as the secretary introduced my availability to deliver services to the people at the agency in a way I will never forget.

"All our good people are seeing clients right now," she stated. "However, we do have a new person we just hired. He's kind of green and I don't know much about him except he's not very good at playing cards. However, if you are really desperate we will send him over. Are you really desperate, ma'am?" The reply was affirmative, and before the secretary and the person she was speaking to could say "Jokers are wild," I was off to the agency about five miles away.

When I arrived I was courteously and skeptically greeted and told that the person I was going to see was literally banging his head into the wall in a room at the end of a hallway. I was offered the opportunity to have someone from the agency go into the room with me if I requested. But I assured everyone that this case was fairly routine in mental health circles (after my introduction by the secretary, I was afraid to admit I hadn't a clue as to what to do). So I entered the room feeling a great kinship for Daniel in the lion's den and yet realizing faith, in this case, would probably not pull me from the jaws of my inadequacies or deliver me from my pride.

To make a long story short, what I found in the room was a middle-aged man with long shaggy hair and faded blue overalls knocking his head quite hard against a cinderblock wall. My previous training would have told me to be empathetic and probe by saying something like, "How does that make you feel?" or to reflect and say something like, "I hear your head going thud, thud, thud against that wall pretty regularly. Tell me about that." However, I was more direct and behavioral and stated, "I'm from the mental health center. If you really want help, stop doing that." He looked at me in a sheepish, stunned manner (as if to say, "Why didn't somebody say that about 20 minutes ago?"), and amazingly enough, he quit.

Sometimes being direct and specific can help you and your clients be realistic and get better. The theory I entered that situation with was alright but my client was all wrong for it. The next semester I enrolled in my first behavioral counseling course. I also listened to my clients even more closely after that, especially their nonverbal language.

chapter | 4

THE LOCKED WARD

Having worked for a mental health center for a few months, I was informed that I and "Nurse Nancy" would regularly start visiting clients from the county who were at the regional mental hospital. The idea was to help them begin to make a transition back to our community. It seemed interesting, and I noticed with amusement that the coffee they served at the hospital was poured into Mellaril cups.

"Nothing to fear," everyone assured me. "Just look straight ahead, trust the experience of the personnel on the locked wards, and stick with more seasoned professional colleagues" (such as, in this case, the nurses). So I entered my first locked ward, close to the side of Nurse Nancy, looking stern like an Army commando and quietly saying repetitively under my breath the 23rd Psalm and the Boy Scout motto.

All went well for about 10 feet. Then a rather large woman from the back of the ward spotted us and with loud shouts and angry motions started coming toward us. I looked to Nurse Nancy for reassurance, but I quickly noticed her eyes were glazed over like a Krispy Kreme donut, and she had what is known in the clinical literature as "tonic immobility." (I could have probably used a gin and tonic myself then, but there was no time.) With the woman closing in and no help in sight, I decided to survive by grabbing the keys from my colleague and escaping. There was just one problem. Nurse Nancy was rigid as a two by four, and being frozen in fright, she was not about to release the keys that would have given me freedom.

Thus, I did the most prudent thing I knew—I ran. I was faster than the woman (thank goodness), and there were strategically located support beams on the ward that I could use to run around and wear her out. Finally orderlies arrived (I now know why they call them orderlies) and peace was restored. Nurse Nancy, still clutching the keys, and I then departed unceremoniously. I was wiser and a bit more frazzled and fatigued than when we arrived. But I also realized the absurdity of what had just happened.

From that experience I learned to stay flexible in counseling and never passively depend on a cocounselor to make the situation better. I also came to realize that sometimes your best asset in counseling may not be your words but your actions, in this case behavior involving my feet. Finally, I learned anew how close the comic and the tragic are to each other. I could have been hurt if I had remained immobile. Instead, by keeping my head and using my legs, I was able to put distance between the woman and me and ultimately to place the incident in perspective.

Points to ponder |

1. What is the story of your becoming a counselor? Was it a planned and systematic process or a result of happenstance?

2. What theory do you ascribe to most closely? Can you imagine a situation in which it was inadequate or not appropriate? What then would you do?

3. When have you ever been surprised by the unfolding of events? What did you learn in that situation?

Section | two

FINDING WHAT WORKS

He changed,
giving her small compliments at breakfast, such as
"I like the way your hair looks" or
"Nice dress."
She wondered,
"What's he doing?"
but she also knew she liked his words.
So as the days continued
she responded to his acts of kindness
with new behaviors of her own.
He changed;
She changed;
They changed.
And it was for the better!

When I began my work as a counselor, I was somewhat sure I knew what worked. I had taken a course under Rollo May and attended lectures by Carl Rogers, Albert Ellis, Virginia Satir, and other notable therapists. Therefore, I was surprised when I struggled sometimes with certain clients whose problems these masters had made look somewhat easy to resolve. Was it me? Was it the theory I was using? Was it the client? Or was it all of the aforementioned factors combining in a dynamic way that my texts, counseling films, and teachers had not explained? I was not sure.

However, I began to realize in time that I could not really emulate any one of the greats I admired. My clients were different from theirs, and I was a person whose history and knowledge also differed. So, from insight came a struggle to take calculated risks and interact with clients in ways that were uniquely my own. In the process, I found interventions that worked and gained confidence and competence. It is in finding what works that we sometimes find our identity and humanity.

chapter | 5

TALK IS CHEAP

From the adamant behaviorist on my doctoral committee (as well as from my clients), I have learned that sometimes an altered action is worth a thousand words. The most blatant example of the power of new behavior occurred in my professional life with a woman who was literally doing nothing in counseling. I would meet with her, and she would ramble. I would confront her rambling, and she would be evasive, explaining to me that she needed to give me details so I could truly understand her. I would then listen again, and she would repeatedly stray. Our sessions seemed to go on forever, and at the end of each, there was nothing to show for the time invested.

Finally, one day in trying to understand the dynamics that were occurring in our sessions, I told her that I thought she was not making progress and that I was concerned. She replied flippantly that she thought counseling was fairly worthless and ended by saying, "And besides, talk is cheap."

I looked at her, somewhat amazed, dazed, and befuddled. I was not particularly offended by the fact that she did not seem to highly value counseling. However, her last statement made me think that I needed to make an intervention so that her perception would have an opportunity to be modified. Thus, I decided to take a risk and an action that I normally would never have considered.

"I'm doubling your fee," I told her.

Well, if you live near Cape Canaveral you know about the noise and fire associated with the launching of rockets. And if you had been in my office that afternoon you would have thought several missiles had taken off from a non-Florida site. The volume and flow of words in our session increased dramatically, and my client came close to blasting off with anger. However, along with a pick up in the sound and heat came a focus in her sentences. She now knew that time was costly, that life does not continue on one course forever, and that language and thoughts can be powerful if directed toward a goal. From that point on, she took off in a direction that had purpose and resulted in her defining and reaching a destination that allowed her to live a more fruitful, exciting, and inviting existence.

Had I taken no action, I can only surmise that she would have stayed stuck, gotten sick, or continued off course in her life. Change came in the form of doing something differently.

chapter | 6

SOCKS

I once had the challenge of working with a woman who swore she would not change. She had been to the best and the brightest of counselors, she stated, and none of them had been helpful. She was fixated on being unhappy. Quite frankly I thought she was coming to me in order to put another notch on her memory of misery the way gunfighters used to notch their guns. However, I was determined, so we started a counseling relationship, and as she predicted I had zero success with her. For every move and suggestion I made, she had a countermove. I probed. I confronted. I reinforced. I reflected. I empathized. Nothing happened. Finally, after several sessions and no progress, I realized the inevitable. She had "won."

Rather than be passive or aggressive about the matter, I became aware that I needed to do something to commemorate the event. Thus, as we were about to end another frustrating session, I reached down, untied my shoes, took off my socks, and handing them to her, I said:

"You have won, and as a symbol of your victory, you shall have my socks. They are the modern equivalent of a sword or a shield that was given in antiquity to the victor at the end of a struggle. I want you to take them and display them on the mantel over your fireplace like a trophy. Then you can tell others of your hard work and what it led to. But please," I said, "just don't mention my name. I have a reputation in the community, and I don't like to admit failure."

She was stunned. She did not want to take the socks, but I was aware that somehow she must. So I persisted and insisted. She laughed. Then she did a strange and wonderful thing: She cried. She cried, and she cried, and she cried. When the tears stopped flowing, the words began to tumble out. She became more in tune with the feelings inside of her and acted on them. We extended that session, and we scheduled more. She got better.

She still has my socks as far as I know. They are somewhere in a glassed frame in her house as a symbol of her transformation.

chapter | 7

TEX RITTER SMITH

One of the lightest and yet most anxious moments in my counseling career came about the time Debbie Boone was singing "You Light Up My Life." You may remember that song, but chances are you are even now trying to forget it. But at the time of the song's initial popularity, I was a counselor in a county mental health center that was housed in a pre-Civil War building that Sherman forgot to burn.

One day at the center a rather large mountain of a man, named Tex, came in for his first appointment. What made him a bit unusual was the fact that he had a gun in a holster strapped to his side. I was upstairs in my office, but my faithful secretary, Sa-rah (she actually pronounced her name "Say-Rah," not Sarah), quickly let me know that Tex and his six shooter had arrived. She was disturbed, and I must admit I had concern, too.

Nevertheless, I came downstairs to find Tex in the waiting room. I introduced myself, shook his hand, and then said to him as he stood up,

"You know, Tex, we don't allow firearms in our counseling sessions. They have a way of frightening the counselors. However, we can arrange to take care of your gun while you and I talk. Come with me."

I then took him over to Sa-rah's desk, gave her one of those knowing winks that means "play along with me here," and said to Tex,

"Sa-rah, our receptionist, used to be a cowgirl. She's from the West you know. Sa-rah, tell Tex where you are from."

Without blinking an eye or seeming to understand anything that was going on, Sa-rah said in a rather monotone voice, "I'm from Mayodan, North Carolina."

Trying to put a good spin on her answer, I replied: "Yes, Mayodan, North Carolina, where the Mayo and Dan Rivers converge, where the deer and the porcupine play, where seldom is heard a discouraging word or much more than wild animal noises. You know, Tex, some people say that Mayodan is where the West really begins. There are no buffalo there, but they do have an ostrich farm. Tex, have you ever tangled with an ostrich?"

Unimpressed, Tex just grunted.

"There's no rapport being built here," I thought, but I continued the conversation, giving Sa-rah a double wink (like help me out a little here will you, Sarah, or we both may die). Then I told Tex that Sa-rah would give him a receipt for his gun.

"She does it for people who have pets, opossums, or other possessions that we think would be better left out of sessions," I said.

Well, as Tex reached for his gun, Sa-rah just stared into space, so I gave her hand motions to start writing something. Finally, she reached for a pink telephone message pad, and as Tex laid down his gun, Sa-rah handed him a pink slip of paper with these words on it:

"While you are away, this is where your gun will stay."

Tex seemed okay with the note, and as luck would have it, we actually had a good session. He never showed up with his firearm again.

From my experience with Sa-rah and Tex that day, I learned that sometimes if you stay fluid and keep the conversation light until it needs to be heavy, you can set up the right conditions in counseling so that your encounters can be productive. Being flexible in the midst of potential danger or difficulty does not mean "shooting from the hip." Rather, it involves timing, patience, and a sensitivity to know that most solutions in life come from interactions you would probably never predict.

chapter | 8

PLAYING HUNCHES

I wish counseling were purely scientific. If it were more like physics or chemistry, I would be more sure of what to do and when to do it. I could use a formula. But because of the gap in research and practice, we, as counselors, must sometimes use our intuition as much as our cognitive knowledge.

That realization occurred to me one day when I was visiting a hospitalized client who was going to have a major operation the next morning. We talked for some time at his bedside about what he had been through therapeutically and what his expectations of the future were. It seemed to me that he had a solid knowledge of reality.

As I was leaving, he said, "I'm not at all worried about tomorrow."

His words made perfect sense. Yet, I was uncomfortable with them. I did not know the reason behind the discomfort, but it was there. Then it dawned on me. It was not what was said but how it was said. My client's words had come out in a bravado manner that made me suspect that he was not as sure of himself as he had conveyed.

Therefore, I made a 180-degree turn in the doorway and reentered the room. "Tom," I said, "While I do not doubt your sincerity, I do have a hunch that what you just said doesn't ring true in your mind."

He laughed for a minute and dismissed my observation with a glib remark or two, but then reaching out for my hand, he confessed, "You're right."

In the next half hour, my client's thoughts and emotions came together. Thus, when I left I knew he was not just pretending to be brave when he said he hoped to see me the next day. Yogi Berra once purportedly made the statement that you can see a lot through observing. He could have also said, had he been a counselor instead of a catcher and coach, that you can hear a lot just by listening, especially if you listen for feelings.

chapter | 9

CONSULTANT OR CATALYST

A consultant is sometimes referred to as someone who blows in, blows off, and blows out. Sometimes that is true, but good consultation occurs when a counselor works with someone else for the benefit of a third party, for example, a client or an organization.

When I worked in a mental health agency I was frequently asked to consult at one of the four local school systems. The asking became so burdensome that I realized I needed to do something to maximize time and effort spent in working with school personnel. Therefore, I invited each of the school systems to send their counselors to the mental health center for a meeting once a month. My thought was that the counselors as a group could help each other and I could orchestrate that process as well as add to it by being a consultant. The plan worked initially. Then some of the more anxious and overwhelmed counselors began to dominate the meetings by asking questions concerning some severe situations.

In order to remedy the situation, I asked our in-house psychiatrist to join the group. At first I thought the group might try to use him like a local advice giver, but instead of seeing him in such a narrow way, they opened up and queried him about a wide range of disorders and dysfunctions. Everyone was fascinated and pleased with the interactive nature of the discussions, and soon there was a request that our monthly meetings become bimonthly. They did, and as they expanded so did the topics covered.

What I noticed out of all of this effort was that I was no longer receiving as many telephone calls or requests to come out to the schools. I also noted counselors gaining greater diagnostic skills and assessment abilities. Furthermore, the counselors in the group became better at working with each other and at formulating plans for the children and parents who populated their offices.

I became a catalyst in the process of being a consultant. The psychiatrist and the counselors had been brought together. Their interaction was dynamic and far-reaching. Everyone won.

chapter | 10

SOMETIMES IT IS HOW YOU ASK THE QUESTION

One of those aspects of counseling that I have become attuned to over the years is the importance of how a question is worded and to whom. Open-ended questions are usually best in eliciting thoughts and feelings, whereas closed-ended questions are most appropriate for obtaining specific information. Likewise, children and those who may be a bit mentally challenged do better with simpler inquiries. However, there is no specific formula for what question is asked and how it is worded. I have found out this fact on numerous occasions, but I will illustrate it with two stories.

My initial experience in realizing the importance of how you ask questions came with a late-adolescent girl who was brought into counseling by her mother. The mother was concerned that the girl was being promiscuous and was going to get into serious trouble. I could see why the mother would get such an idea because of the way her daughter was dressed. A low neckline and a high hemline were invitations for trouble at her age, especially if she was flirtatious. However, I did not want to appear to side with the mother immediately and thought I needed to say something to the girl in order to establish rapport. Trying to begin on a positive note, I asked,

"Jenny, what do other people say is your most outstanding quality?"

Without blinking, she replied, "I'm 115 pounds of romping, stomping sex."

All I could do then was say, "Besides sex, Jenny, what is your best quality?" That question resulted in an answer that was more productive, but by then she was in the doghouse and my face was scarlet.

Another time, I also made a probe that could have been better phrased. I was getting ready to lead a group, and I thought I would ask my wife, Claire, a question I was going to use in the group to see how it would work.

"Honey," I said, "What group in your life gave you hope?"

"The Eagles" she replied in a straightforward manner.

Before I could explain to her that I was not talking about rock-and-roll groups (which I frequently did around the house), she said, "Yeah. It was their song 'Desperado' that really spoke to me. Those lyrics that 'you better let somebody love you before it's too late' made me wake up more to my life and my relationships. Aren't you glad?!"

Well, I was glad because the song had entered her life before I did and probably had a positive impact on the development of our relationship. Yet, it was not quite what I was looking for when I asked the question. So, the next day as I began the group I made a clarifying statement as such:

"Besides a singing group, what group in your life gave you hope?"

The responses were much more of what I had in mind, and the outcome of the group was good because the question had been refined and tailored.

chapter | 11

THREE ACRES OF GARLIC

I normally greet clients by introducing myself, shaking their hands (if appropriate), and asking them to tell me something about themselves. All usually goes smoothly. However, once after the introduction and handshake, my client, a rather burly man, said, "I just want you to know that I'm as strong as three acres of garlic."

I thanked him for the information and sank back in my green-cushioned chair wondering where to begin. So I said, "Mr. Garlic, what brings you here?" He was not humored and replied, "I hate my wife. She's been having an affair. I caught her, and I've now thrown her out of the house. I'm thinking about what to do next. I want revenge."

To put it mildly, I'm convinced that revenge is every bit as strong as love. I am also aware that trying to dissuade someone from seeking revenge directly is often not profitable (even though it is a legally prudent action). So in this case, I asked my client to explain the details around his thoughts and tried to stay cognitive and factual with him. He was unclear about what he was going to do, which was a good sign. Nevertheless, I also had him promise not to do anything violent until he saw me the next day. Then I asked him to do some homework for the next day. "Find someone else who has been hurt in a love relationship," I said, "and tell me what the person did that helped."

The assignment was a gamble because there are many negative models, especially in movies, who resort to less than productive behaviors when they get hurt. I was equally afraid that he might pick up on some less than positive country music and decide to never get over his pain. The next day, however, when my client arrived he had an audiocassette tape in his hand. "Here," he said, "play this song." To my surprise, the tape was by Don Henley, and the song he asked me to play was "Heart of the Matter." As the song progressed, the emotions in my client increased. They finally broke in a cascade of tears when Henley sang, "But I think it's about forgiveness, forgiveness, forgiveness, even though you don't love me anymore."

The words spoke to my client's pain and simultaneously gave him an option for acting that he would not have readily accepted from me. My client followed his heart in listening to his feelings, but he took his lead for constructive action from a singer who verbalized emotions and talked about a way out of despair—"forgiveness." Just as the literature in counseling reminds us, sometimes the best we can do is to be aware of what we cannot do and thereby help our clients find alternative resources for themselves by looking into books, movies, and music that promote positive interactions and solutions.

chapter | 12

THE WORDS ARE THERE/I DON'T KNOW WHERE

She grew up in a family in which there was rampant alcohol abuse and neglect. So although she was polite and attractive, her self-concept was quite low. When she came to me, at the age of 23, she had already been through two marriages and numerous bad relationships. Therefore, she was hesitant to talk. After all, I was another man in her life, a life in which men had been and basically still were diabolical.

Yet, even in the first session I sensed that she knew I was genuinely interested in helping her. There was a glimmer of trust in her eyes. So at the end of the session I said,

"Do you write?"

Her eyes brightened and widened. "Yes," she quietly replied.

"Well, how about writing some of your thoughts this week. You could read them to me next time and that way you would not have to depend on me for questions. You would be in charge." She agreed.

The next week she came in with a couplet that she read to start the session.

The words are there
I don't know where.

To my surprise and I think hers too, she then began to talk about how hard it was to talk. She was especially reluctant to discuss herself, she said, because she really was not important. Yet, she talked about herself, and as her words came out the conversation deepened. Thus, from the initial couplet came thoughts, feelings, and experiences.

She continued to write and became even more spontaneous and open in her speech, especially about herself. Her candor produced clarity, and for the first time in her life she was able to see herself as something other than a victim.

At our last session, she brought in a final couplet. It read as follows:

As I now enjoy and experience the earth
I feel as if I've gone through a total rebirth.

Indeed, she had. Writing led to relaxation, which led to insight, which led to openness and growth. The power of the words helped her raise herself out of despair and depression. Jotting down thoughts is like jogging down trails. Both are therapeutic for those seeking to live healthy lives.

chapter | 13

THE MUSIC OF LIFE

I once worked with a young man who played the guitar for a hobby. I asked him in our intake if there was anything he wanted to say with the guitar because his speech was limited. He said he would think about it, and in the next session, he came in with the guitar and simply said, "Listen."

Then he played some of the most dramatic music I have heard from a guitar. It started off quietly but reached a crescendo that was loud, off-key, and unsettling.

"That's my life," he said after the piece was concluded.

Seizing the moment, I replied, "On which note would you like to begin?"

He picked a section most on his mind at the time and we were off. He would play and then talk. We would look at variations on themes, tunes that sounded similar, and the rhythmic or arrhythmic quality of his selection. He would try some new chords on occasion and vary the beat of a piece. For weeks he brought in his guitar, and we worked through his life as depicted in music. Interestingly enough, not only did the music became mellower in our sessions, but he came to be in greater harmony with his surroundings—and himself—as well.

In the celebration that ended our final session, he again said: "Listen." As I did I could not help but smile as he gleefully played and sang with great feeling the song Frank Sinatra made famous: "My Way."

chapter | 14

KNOWLEDGE IS POWER UP TO A POINT

Once in my career, I taught psychology in a small college in what can only be described as a rural and somewhat "remote" part of the state in which I was living. One of those courses in which I gave instruction was abnormal psychology—a class always filled to the brim with fascinating material and curious students, some of whom too often displayed traits on which I was lecturing. One young man, whom I shall call "Anonymous," particularly stands out in my memory of those times because of his language patterns, his rather well-intentioned but bizarre actions, and what he taught me about change.

To give you a brief glimpse of the young man in question, I will simply say that he tried to talk as if he were hip and often used the word "man" as a preface to opening his remarks. He almost seemed a throwback to the 1960s, but I taught him much later. Regardless, after a particularly intense class on mental disorders and families, he approached me with an excited and seemingly enlightened facial expression. I thought maybe he would comment on the intricate nature of some of the research we had covered, but alas my initial hopes were dashed.

"Man," he said, "I learned a lot today."

I smiled confidently (silently giving myself a compliment and a pat on the back) as I stood before him, hands across my chest, trying to look wise.

"I don't know if you know it," he said, "but you described my family today."

I winced a bit in my mind, shuffled my feet back and forth, and assured him I did not know any of his relatives.

"No problem, man," he said, "I now am aware that I live in an abnormal household with really messed up parents and a sister who is just bizarre. I am going home tonight to tell my family what is wrong with them."

Before I could get a word in edgewise, like "don't," he wheeled around and with the speed of a sprinter, he was gone down the hall, through the doors, and into what I felt like was certain trouble.

The next day, my worst fears for the young man seemed to have materialized. I saw him in the halls looking bedraggled, dazed, and downcast. His backpack seemed full, and his face was flushed. Trying to find out what had happened and to simultaneously establish rapport, I approached him slowly and said,

"Man, how'd it go with you and your family yesterday?"

He looked up at me and with a slight smile that reminded me of colleagues of mine in the Army who had been in the heat of combat. He then replied,

"Fine, fine, fine—at first."

"Yea, man," he continued, "I went in there and told my father he was paranoid, schizoid, and had a character that was disordered. Then I confronted my mother with the fact that she was histrionic, inadequate, and in the words of Linda Ronstadt, I yelled 'you're no good, you're no good, you're no good, mother, you're no good.' Finally, I went in my sister's room and told her she was mentally challenged, unstable, and a disgrace to the human race. Yea, man, I really let them have it."

Then he paused and looked down.

"So, man," I said, "what happened next?"

Sheepishly he said, "Well, man, I'd really prefer not to tell you, but man, do you know anyplace where I can live? They kicked me out of the house."

Knowledge is power, but in the young man's case he became confused about what to do with the limited power he possessed. Knowledge is best when it is used to help people become aware of and sensitive to who they are in regard to others as well as who others are in reference to them . . . and what reality is.

Points to ponder |

1. When have you found it better to listen than to talk? Be specific in fleshing out an example.

2. Write down several open-ended questions and the answers you would expect to receive. Ask the questions to a few friends and observe whether any of the questions need to be refined.

3. When have you found comfort or support in listening to music or reading a book? How did you use what you learned?

Section | three

LEARNING FROM FAILURE

She went about kissing frogs
for in her once-upon-a-time mind
that's what she had learned to do.
With each kiss came expectations
of slimy green changing to well-bleached white.
With each day came realizations
that fly-eating, quick tongued, croaking creatures
don't magically turn to instant princes
from the aftereffects of a fast-smooching,
smooth-talking, helping beauty.
So with regret she came back from a lively lily pond
to the sobering stacks of the village library
To page through the well-worn stories again
and find in print what she knew in fact
that even loved frogs sometimes stay frogs
no matter how pretty the damsel or how high the hope.

—Gladding, 1976[1]

No one likes to fail or taste the bitterness of defeat. Yet, in losing sometimes we gain. I have found that true in a number of arenas in life, including counseling. On the one hand, it is humbling not to live up to the standards that you have set for yourself as a professional. On the other hand, it is human also. At such moments, there is an opportunity not so much to criticize oneself but to constructively learn.

The stories in this section are all about learning. The experiences were hard lessons but ones that have stayed with me and stood the test of time. They may be similar to events you have had or will have, but hopefully you can "go to school" through reading this material and not repeat the mistakes I made. Part of being an effective counselor is preparation, but even the most prepared counselor encounters the unexpected. Ask yourself as you read these vignettes how, if you had been the counselor, you could have avoided making the missteps I did. Also query yourself as to ways you could ethically interact with the situations presented in these snapshots of sessions and slices of life.

chapter | 15

SLEEPY TIME CLIENT

I once worked with an accountant as a client who was incredibly dull. He would come and talk about his relationships in such detail that I found my mind drifting. Therefore, I used to take two cups of strong coffee into our sessions. One was for me. The other was for him in case he began boring himself. As fate would have it, one day the appointment was on, but the coffee pot was off. I had cups but no java. There we were, my client and I, face to face, with no stimulants to help us.

I tried. I really made an effort to stay awake and to be active. I moved around initially and used every technique I knew. But finally his monotone, flat-affect voice, and his propensity for using 10 words when 1 would do, wore me down. Before you could say "deep sleep," I had sunk into the comfort of my chair only to be awakened by my own snoring.

As I woke up in a startle, I could see he was not pleased. I was, to say the least, extremely embarrassed. I thought of saying, "My kids kept me up late last night and I am tired," or trying to appease him by saying, "I'm sorry and you don't have to pay for today's session." However, believing that honest self-disclosure can be powerful and productive, I made a confession.

"Ralph," I said, "I regret having gone to sleep during our session. I have never gone to sleep during a counseling session before. This is truly a first. But, Ralph, if I did this while trying to listen, I wonder what might be happening in your other relationships where people are not necessarily attempting to be so close."

He looked at me, and to my surprise, he quietly said, "I really don't have any other relationships. That's why I'm here. When I tell you I have friends, they are mostly mental. I am lonely. I am unloved. And I want to stop fooling myself and you."

From then on, the details stopped and the feelings started. I did not have to depend on the coffee pot, and Ralph did not have to depend on me to be his friend. The sleep of embarrassment woke up both of us to new possibilities, thanks to honest and appropriate self-disclosure.

chapter | 16

BO: A DISASTER IN ASSESSMENT

Part of my life as a counselor has been spent doing assessments. Some of these assessments have been completed in the offices in which I worked, whereas others have occurred in a school environment. I must confess to liking my office better than school offices because I have found there is no standard place to test in some schools. I have also realized over the years that rapport and relationships (not to mention scores) are sometimes negatively affected when I am on the road.

The most sobering experience I had in this regard was with a first grader whom I shall call "Bo." He was a light-skinned African American boy who had a wiry build. The principal brought him to me and said he wanted Bo assessed because Bo did not seem able to settle down like the rest of the children and do his lessons. I had my standardized testing instruments with me, but I did not have a place to test. Therefore, I asked in the presence of Bo (because he was already there) where we were to conduct the assessment. The principal had not really thought ahead. However, he led us to the nurse's office, which was a glassed-in area that had the nurse's name on the outside of the door and was furnished with a bed, a desk, and two chairs. It would have to do. With that he left.

I immediately recognized the difficulty of the environment and the fact that Bo did not know me. Therefore, I thought I would try to establish rapport and create a positive atmosphere before I did anything else. I told Bo who I was and what we would be doing. I also asked him to tell me about himself (but at age 6 he had nothing to say).

Realizing the nonverbal nature of young children, I said, "Bo, I have a puppet here in my materials I want to show you." Then I reached down and behind me to retrieve the sock puppet I had brought for such occasions.

The next thing I heard was the sound of a slamming door. Bo had bolted and was literally running down the hallway bouncing off the walls in a zigzag fashion like a ball in a pinball machine. I was shocked but instantly on my feet. I quickly opened the door and tore down the halls running after Bo. He was easy to follow because of the sounds he was making and the course he was taking, but he was fast and the chase seemed to go on forever. I finally caught Bo in front of the principal's office where the principal was standing, watching these actions unfold. He was not pleased nor were the teachers who came into the halls to see what had happened after hearing Bo blow quickly past their classrooms in a disruptive manner. I was exhausted and I knew Bo was, too, so we ended our session that day. Exhaustion had taken its toll.

Driving back to the office with the memories of the time, I thought that before I entered a school again for an evaluation I would call first to make sure they had a place for me to set up. I also knew that in advance of seeing a child (or an adult for that matter) for an assessment, I would be sure I had sufficient background information and would not depend on disinterested personnel to find a place for me to work. I also realized that materials used in an evaluation from sock puppets to scoring sheets should always be as close as possible and preferably out in front or to the side of you.

chapter 17

RABBITS

I had completed intake information on a man and asked him what he would like to work on in the session. He looked at me a bit negatively and simply stated, "I am not talking until you get rid of the rabbits in this room."

We were in a rural area so I surveyed our surroundings. Not seeing any rabbits, I asked where they were. He pointed to an imaginary hare (that I assumed was wild), and I went over, grabbed it by its invisible ears, then opened the door, and threw it outside. As I went to sit down he pointed to a second nonvisible bunny, so I proceeded to do the same thing. Again, as I went back to my chair he pointed to a third unseeable furry critter with long ears and a cotton tail (so he said). As I approached this third imaginary rabbit and started to grab it by its airy ears, I suddenly stopped and thought, as I bent down, "Just who really needs help here?"

From the experience I came to realize and appreciate anew that if counseling is going to be beneficial, it must be based in reality. I gave up doing for clients what I thought they expected and learned to confront. I probably would have eventually learned to do these and other necessary helping techniques in counseling, but my client experience sped up the process. It helped me know that there was much I needed to do if I was not going to get lost in the history of being an outdated counselor in a postmodern world.

chapter | 18

TESTING A THEORY: THE SOUND OF SILENCE

In my counseling program, I thought I learned one theory well: person-centered. Its origin was in the writings of the theorist Carl Rogers. I thought it had a lot of merit, and as a novice counselor, I imagined it would be easy to implement. The major part of it seemed to me to be reflection. If I could reflect well enough I thought my clients would get better sooner because they would be able to hear their thoughts and feelings and become more congruent.

If some reflection was good, would not more be better? Thus one day I resolved to "out-Roger" Carl Rogers and become the most reflective counselor east of the Mississippi River. By nightfall, I thought, a number of clients would be much better off because of my stance. At 10 a.m. came the perfect opportunity to initiate my beliefs, for at that hour not only did I have my first appointment for the day but it was with a teenage girl.

"Who likes to talk more than teenage girls?" I wondered. "This young woman will naturally talk," I thought, "and as I reflect she will become more insightful into herself and begin to make choices and changes."

Unfortunately for me, the young woman who came to my office that day was as silent as light. She had been referred, and she did not want to see me or anybody else. Nevertheless, I put forth my best Rogerian style. I empathized with her situation and told her I was there to listen and reflect with her. She was not impressed. Instead of talking, she sat. I sat with her, hoping to reflect being open, interested, and respectful. None of it worked. The harder I tried, the more trying it was. Finally, after about 15 minutes of silence, which seemed like an eternity, I asked her if she had anything to say since she had been mute for most of our time together.

"Yes," was her reply. "I want to go now."

"Out the door?"

"Precisely."

Then she left, and the only thing I felt was the breeze from her passing by my chair and a strange emptiness inside. I had failed.

I had been more like Roy Rogers than Carl Rogers. The result was that nothing happened.

After that time, I focused more on being myself. I did not forget theories. In fact, I tried to learn them better. I used them as models and adapted them in line with published research. My counseling became much improved.

chapter | 19

BE MODEST

People who seek counseling do so for many reasons. Some believe you can help them sort out their personal and career concerns, and they are usually right. Others, however, believe you can work miracles such as making them motivated, insightful, and successful. They are usually sincere in these beliefs but wrong. Before I became a counselor, I found out the importance of modesty and its impact on expectations.

I was in divinity school at the time. I had broken my ankle in an intramural game of volleyball in December, so instead of driving back to school I took a plane after the semester break. The first leg of the trip went well as I flew from my home in Atlanta to New York City aboard a spacious jet. However, the second leg of my trip was much harder. My flight from New York to New Haven, Connecticut, where I was studying, was aboard a single-engine plane with three seats. The pilot had one, I had the other, and a heavyset woman easily occupied the rest of the remaining space. The woman was pleasant, and we soon established rapport and struck up a conversation. In the middle of our talk she asked me what I was currently doing, and I made the mistake of telling her with some enthusiasm and probably a bit of pride that I was studying theology.

Then it happened! Over the Long Island Sound, the engine suddenly quit. It went dead, and all we could hear around us was the silence of air as we glided along briefly for a moment in the eerie pretense that nothing was wrong. Yet in that instant, I looked at my fellow passenger and she at me. Then, reaching out with two meaty hands, she grabbed me by my tie, pulled me up to her face, and with a brief but forceful breath she uttered just one word: "Pray."

I wanted to tell her that I could not breathe, let alone pray. I also wanted to thank her for choking me to death so I would not drown. Yet, before I could do any of these things, the engine started, and she dropped me to the floor like a stone. With the release, I regained my composure, said a little prayer, moved as far away from the woman as I could, and vowed to always be modest from then on in how I presented myself and what I did.

Since that time, I have found that if expectations of clients in regard to who you are and what you can do are not too high, they are usually better off and so are you.

chapter | 20

A DOOR, A PHONE, A WINDOW

I grew up trusting people, and that attitude toward others spilled over into counseling. However, it might have been better for me initially had it not been so. The reason is the way I arranged the first office I did not share with others. The office was an elongated room with cinder brick walls. Because of its shape, I had to place my desk and chairs in less than ideal ways in order to make best use of the space. In the process I placed the desk at the front of the room near the door with the phone on it, placed my clients' chairs next, and finally put my chair closest to the window. "I'll enjoy the view and the fresh air more if I sit here," I thought.

And so I did for several months. However, as fate would have it, one day I was asked to see a very disturbed client for an evaluation. I could tell on encountering him that the task was not going to be easy. Nevertheless, I asked him to follow me to my office. On arriving I motioned for him to sit where my clients usually did. I, in turn, took my seat. About two minutes later, I realized I was in trouble. The disheveled man was becoming agitated and hostile. He was verbally threatening and was big enough to be physically intimidating.

I needed help, but the client was between me, the door, and the phone. I had a problem. I tried everything I knew to calm him and the situation, but things steadily grew worse. There was no way to finesse my way past the client, and he was moving in the wrong direction, toward me. Thus, I headed toward the window. It was unlocked and opened easily. I was out of it in the twinkling of an eye and not a second too soon. It was a relief when I hit the ground, but I did not stop to congratulate myself for surviving the drop of about four feet. Instead, I went to get help and entered the front of the building where I greeted our surprised receptionist.

"I thought you were in with a client," she said.

"I was," I replied, "but I had to leave." Then I quickly explained to her what was happening and she went to the phone to do her duty. Soon the emergency medical personnel arrived and my client was calmed.

Although I was a bit embarrassed about being a counselor dropout that day, I went to school on the experience. The next morning, the phone on the desk came closer to my chair and within easy reach should an emergency arise. My chair moved too and became situated between my client and the door. The window remained where it was.

chapter | 21

THE PRICE OF BEING ILL-PREPARED

When I did my initial graduate school work at Yale University, one day I went out for a ride with a friend. We went along an unmarked route in the rolling hill country of western Connecticut and had a wonderful time exploring the Nutmeg State. However, as we attempted to return at dusk, we made one wrong turn after another as we tried to figure out (without a map) where we were and how we would get back to our residence hall.

As if we were not suffering enough for our folly of being ill-prepared, my friend who was driving made an illegal turn across a busy highway in front of a Connecticut State Highway Patrol car. Needless to say, the sharp eyes of the trooper in the car spotted us, and soon we had been pulled over with the state trooper on the driver's side of the car talking to my friend.

"You can't make a left turn like that," the trooper said.

To which my friend replied, "That's not true. I just did."

My friend was correct. He knew what he had done, and he wanted to assure the officer that it was possible. Unfortunately, the possible was also illegal and had a fine attached to it. Some hours later when we finally reached our destination, my friend said in summing up our day,

"Getting lost costs a lot."

Likewise in counseling, there is a high price associated with poor preparation or illegal behavior. Such action takes us and our clients down the wrong roads or in the wrong directions. The result is that time, energy, resources, abilities, and hope are wasted that can never be recovered.

chapter | 22

THE WRONG SIDE OF PRESENTATIONS

Part of one's professional responsibility is to attend and make presentations on clinical aspects of counseling. It is much easier to attend than to present.

In order to present, you not only have to formulate ideas but also develop them in such a way that others find your words interesting and informative. There are several ways I have found that produce certain failure.

First, if you do not want people coming back to ever hear you again, become a part of a large, uncoordinated group that merely lectures to those in attendance. I did this once and only once. I was part of a panel at an American Counseling Association convention. Each of the presenters was a notable and quotable type of person, but we had not rehearsed. When the program was over, a young man came up to me and said, "Who was responsible for this program?"

Being modest I replied, "Well, all of us really, but I organized it."

"It was awful," he said. "You guys need to get your act together." With that, he walked away, and I woke up to the reality that he was right.

The second way not to be successful as a presenter is to find out as little as you can about your audience. I again made such a mistake at a large university gathering where I was making a presentation on groups. Instead of finding out what participants knew about the subject, who they were, or what their interests were, I plunged right in with my prepared remarks. No one fell out of a chair into the aisle in a dead faint or started foaming at the mouth, but the presentation was less than a success. No one was connected with each other or me. Thus, the words I spoke lost their relevance and potency.

A final guideline for being unsuccessful in presenting is to stay completely cognitive and talk in a monotone. I am not a monotone type of guy as a rule, but I confess to once being completely so at a state counseling convention. I did not stray from my prepared remarks. However, my audience strayed mentally (and some physically) from the room. The sound of hard syllables crashing together can be deafening and demoralizing.

As I said initially, it is easier to attend than present at a conference. But presentations have multiple payoffs in the ways they stimulate thinking and lead to the discovery of new knowledge and friendships. The secret of such outcomes, however, is being well prepared and preparing audiences as well. An old rock-and-roll group used to be called the Monotones, but it is not a name we want to be called as counselors, especially during presentations.

chapter | 23

LEARNING THE LINGO

Part of being an effective counselor involves understanding, not just hearing, a client's words. Otherwise, all kinds of mischief may occur.

The importance of understanding language was initially called to my attention when I was a graduate student at Yale. On the first morning of class, a friend from New Jersey said to me, "Let's go get a Danish."

Taken aback, I replied, "Can we and why would we want to?" (I had no desire to intentionally go after someone from Scandinavia.)

He was as surprised by my remark as I was by his. However, he insisted, and before you could say "sugar topping" we stood in front of a pastry shop in downtown New Haven.

"So what kind of Danish do you want?" he said as we gazed at the goodies in the window.

"I don't see any Danish," I replied.

"Well," a bit exasperated he said, "what do you call those things right in front of your eyes?"

"Sweet rolls," I responded (for that is what they were called in my native state of Georgia).

"Oh," was all he could say. "Here we call them Danish." Then we walked into the shop with a better understanding of each other and the power of words.

In counseling, two similar situations concerning language stand out in my memory. In one, my client kept talking about "busting" the soil. What he meant was he needed to plow. In the second (I'm embarrassed to say), a teenage girl I was counseling mentioned that the night before she had "smoked a roach" and that it had nearly "drove" her crazy.

"I can imagine it would," I remember saying. "Roaches are not clean insects."

Only after she stopped laughing did I realize she had not lit up a brown creepy creature that is the scourge of people everywhere. Instead she had inhaled the last drags of a marijuana "cigarette."

Listening is only as powerful as one's ability to understand.

chapter | 24

THE WAKE-UP DREAM

My initial experience on the importance of interaction in learning came as a result of a class I taught in which I was an adjunct instructor. The course was an introduction to psychology that met at 8 a.m. at a local community college. I worked hard on the course because I hoped to someday become a professor. However, the class schedule was against me because I did not believe in life before 10 a.m. (and my students apparently did not either).

My limited knowledge of the subject was also a drawback. And to make matters worse, my method of delivery was disastrous. I lectured every day with all the pizzazz of a drone bee in autumn. I realized after about the fifth class session that I was boring my students, but I continued to hope they would finally find the material and me interesting. Alas, it did not happen.

Then one night after working on my notes into the wee hours, I fell asleep and had a dream. In it, I saw my students lining up in front of my desk, with me standing on top of the desk behind a lecturn. Like ducks in a carnival shooting gallery, each student came by and would tilt his or her head backward. I would grab a sheet of lecture material, place it over his or her mouth, and with a cannon ramrod that was close by, stuff the material down the student's gullet. It was a scene full of pressure, frustration, and absurdity.

The intensity of the dream woke me up. In my awareness of the moment I knew I had a choice. I could continue as I was and the class atmosphere would degenerate, or I could try something (almost anything) new. I opted for the latter. The next day I had the class circle up in a group and began by sharing the dream with them. That was the start of our first group discussion. It was a satisfying and sensitive experience for us all. It would never have happened if I had dismissed the awareness of the dream and called it a nightmare. Instead, I gave up an old way of working and tried something new. The interactive nature of the working relationship that resulted with the class was worth making.

Points to ponder |

1. When have you failed in something you tried? What did you learn from it? How have you changed since then?

2. In your studies or travels, have you ever been ill-prepared? What happened? What did you do differently after that?

3. What words or descriptive terms have you learned in recent years? How did this new language help you better understand yourself and your environment?

Section | four

SKILLS AND PROCESSES

She works in a world I have never known
full of rainbow pills and lilac candles
woven together with simple time-stitches
a pattern of color in a gray fabric factory
where she spends her days spinning threads
that go to Chicago by night.
Once with a little girl smile and a giggle
she flew to Atlanta in her mind,
opening the door to instant adventure
far from her present fatigue.
That was a journey we shared
arranging her thoughts in patchwork patterns
until the designs and desires came together.

—Gladding, 1974[2]

As counselors we bring special knowledge and skills into our interactions with others. We are aware of human growth and development as well as clinical pathology. We are also informed as to what skills work best with which clients and when. Therefore, when we are working with clients, part of our focus is on the processes we will use to help them get beyond the places where they are stuck so that they do not get or remain sick but rather grow.

In the vignettes in this section, the focus is on skills and processes that lead us as people and professionals to make needed choices and changes in regard to what we are doing. It is crucial, as the story "Afraid of Blood" implies, that we make sure we help clients keep their lives and actions in perspective even when they are getting better. Skills and processes are tools, and we as counselors must use them carefully.

chapter | 25

THE BASICS

In counseling, the basics are important. This fact came home to me one day in an experience with my oldest son, Ben, when he was three years old. At that time, we had moved into a new house with a banister on the second-floor landing. One day soon after the move, Ben put his head through the banister railings and began to cry as he struggled to get free. His cries brought his mother to the rescue. She pulled, pushed, greased his head with oil, and did all within her power to help him escape his entrapment. But, alas, her efforts were in vain.

Finally, as my wife was about to cut the banister railings, she said in exasperation, "How did you ever get yourself caught like this?"

The boy's reply was to raise his head up and wiggle his body through the rails back to the landing so that he was free once more. "Like this," he said, as he retraced his steps. To his surprise and to the delight of his mother, he had helped himself by remembering the basics of how he got to where he was in the first place.

As counselors we depend on basic knowledge and skills. Part of that knowledge is remembering to not do a client's work for him or her and to stay cognizant of where we have been in our sessions as well as where we are going.

chapter | 26

THE DIFFICULTY OF CHANGE

Change is a critical element in counseling, but it does not always come easy. We are creatures of habit, and once a routine is established, the pattern—even if it is dysfunctional—is hard to break. For example, people in abusive situations often tend to stay in them rather than leave because they prefer a known environment and a predictable pattern of behavior to what is unknown. The difficulty of change has been one I have seen throughout my career, but it was initially demonstrated to me, at least on a mechanical level, when I was a somewhat financially strapped and struggling graduate student.

I needed to make a local telephone call. The cost for such calls then was a dime. I had a quarter. Thus, as I picked up the receiver in the telephone booth, I wondered if I would receive change back if I deposited my coin. I did not have to ponder the question long. Above the phone were information and instructions from the company. One sentence near the end of this material read,

"This phone does not give change."

Under the sentence was one scrawled in black ink from a disgruntled customer, I am sure, that read,

"It doesn't even try!"

So I found out, on that day at least, that my wishes for change were not going to be fulfilled. Therefore, I talked for as long as I could on the call I made to hopefully get my money's worth and then some. However, the more important lesson that I took from the experience and that I have since applied to counseling is that some people are more like the telephone I called from than others. Those who do not try do not change, despite our wishes or skills.

chapter | 27

THE PACE OF CHANGE

When my children were young, they used to enjoy gathering their loose change and wrapping similar coins together. The process was educational and fun. It even became ritualized at one time into a family affair, and Fridays became "wrap nights." After our wrapping, I would take the rolls of coins to the campus bank on Mondays to make an exchange and bring back dollar bills in return.

One time, however, this ordeal got a bit out of hand. The children had saved up more than usual, and instead of several rolls of coins, I ended up carrying $56 worth of silver and copper (mostly pennies) onto campus one day. My coat and pants pockets were stuffed. To make matters worse, I could not find a parking space near the campus bank. Thus, as fate would have it on that hot summer morning, I got out of my car filled with determination but loaded down with heavy metal. After a few steps, I felt myself wobble. The task was more than I had envisioned. My movement became slower, and my knees began to buckle just slightly as I bent toward the ground like a tree during a windstorm. Still I continued with a swaying motion.

However, just as the bank entered my sight so did an important university official. Because I was not moving fast and was slouched over, he quickly overtook me, and with a worried look on his face, he said, "Sam, what's wrong?"

Not wanting him to think I was being frivolous in regard to my regular duties and yet not wanting to be less than truthful about the coins I was carrying, I replied, "I think I've just become overwhelmed by change."

Indeed, I had. I was trying to carry too much, and instead of being engaged in a fun process, I was now struggling to just keep going. The same is true with change for clients and colleagues. They usually do best when they (and we) do not try to do everything at the same time. Small change is manageable. Too much change, all at once, can be debilitating.

chapter | 28

BOUNDARIES: AN AWAKENING

It was 2 a.m. when the phone rang. I had been asleep for approximately three hours. Therefore, I was not quite sure whether the ringing I heard was from a dream within my head or from an outside stimulus. However, in a somewhat groggy manner, I picked up the phone receiver and muttered a "hello."

"Dr. Gladding," a perky female voice on the other end sang out, "this is Jane. Remember me? I'm one of your clients."

"Yes."

"Well," she continued, "I know it's 2 a.m., but I just can't get to sleep tonight." Her voice was almost cheerful.

"Jane, what have you tried doing to get to sleep?"

"Nothing," she said somewhat gleefully. "I'm just not sleeping so I thought I'd call you and talk."

"Jane, I don't know if this will shock you, but I can sleep. In fact, just now I was sleeping quite well. I would suggest you try to get some sleep. If you can't, please call the emergency number I gave you. If you want to call the office tomorrow, I am sure we can arrange an appointment soon." With that, I hung up, rolled over, and went back to sleep.

The next morning Jane arranged an appointment and came to see me. After that time, she no longer called me late at night or at home. Although my behavior may have initially seemed to be rude to her, it set a boundary regarding our relationship.

Most boundaries can and should be set through using a professional disclosure statement during the first session of counseling. If boundaries are not set, clients can become intrusive and inappropriately interrupt your private life. When that happens you as a counselor will lose more than sleep, and no one will be helped in the long run.

chapter | 29

MODELING: A CASE OF STARLINGS

"I'm afraid of starlings," she said. "They swoop down so low and so fast that I am fearful they will peck me on the head or fly into my face and I will be injured."

I sat there nodding, my head was shaking up and down, but my mind was trying to comprehend what my client was talking about. So I responded with an investigative comment. "Tell me more."

"Well, I don't know exactly anything else to say. I'm just scared, and since I live on a farm, I am finding my life unpleasant. I'm afraid to walk outside to the barn."

"Has anyone you know had a starling peck them on the head or fly into their face?"

"No."

"Are there a lot of incidents that you've read about where people were hurt by starlings?"

Once again the answer was negative.

However, the facts were not sufficient. My client was still fearful. I could see it in her eyes and hear it in her voice. I was not going to talk her out of her fear.

"How far away from here is your farm?"

"About a 15-minute drive," she said.

"Well, how about if we go for a visit now and see these starlings?"

"Okay," she responded, and we were out the door and into her car as quickly as a bird on the wing.

When we reached the farm, we initially stayed in the car as she pointed the birds out to me.

"Let's go for a walk," I suggested in my best invitational voice.

She shook her head from side to side.

"Okay," I said. "I'll go walk and you watch."

I did and she did.

Sure enough the starlings swooped down low near my head like dive-bombers in a World War II movie. They came in swiftly, but they seemed to have a sense of space and place. They came close but never really came that near to where I felt I had to fear for my safety. The first day ended with my client watching.

However, the next session, which was held at the farm again, was one in which she participated after seeing me walk around the barn once by myself. She joined me, and as we strolled we talked about the nature of starlings swooping down to get insects stirred up by people or animals. She was still scared but less so than before.

Later sessions were spent in similar ways with me videotaping her and showing her how the birds reacted to her. She then started studying herself as much as she did the birds' movements. The result was an action she called the "bird walk" where she showed me how she could move in such a way that she was comfortable with herself in the presence of starlings.

It was through seeing that she came into believing that she need not be afraid of starlings. Counseling is sometimes a profession of demonstrations. We need to model and often lead by example before we can expect any differences in our clients. Change does not come through reason, knowledge, or even insight alone. It is a process in which actions can and often do speak louder than words.

chapter | 30

MR. TBA: THE IMPORTANCE OF KNOWING OTHERS

The importance of establishing rapport in a relationship with others came when I was an instructor at a community college across the street from the mental health center where I worked. Because I was not asked to teach until a couple of days before the term began, the college had simply noted that under "Introduction to Psychology," the instructor would be named later and had done so with the traditional abbreviation "TBA" (to be announced). Well, as fate would have it, on the opening day of class one of my students was late. She came in about halfway through the class and quietly slid into a blue plastic desk chair in the only place left—at the front of the room. When I finished my remarks for the day and as the class was leaving, I caught the eye of the tardy student and asked her to see me for a minute so I could give her a syllabus. Being new to the college and having missed introductions, when she approached me, she said,

"I'm really sorry I was late, Mr. TBA. I had car trouble. By the way, what kind of name is TBA? Is it Italian? My ancestors were from Italy, you know."

Well after she realized my name was not TBA and I was not Italian, and she had her assignments for the term, she went away disappointed but aware of our relationship and how it would play out. Although this example is a bit silly, it illustrates, I hope, the importance of initial introductions and that establishing rapport with people is crucial to developing relationships with them both inside and outside of counseling. Rapport building is never based on assumptions alone or on printed facts.

chapter | 31

EMPATHY

Empathy, as Carl Rogers once said, is the ability to enter the private world of someone else and be thoroughly at home in it. It is a quality that makes a difference in whether our clients change or not.

When I first learned about empathy, I thought it would be a skill that would come naturally to counselors and those seeking to be counselors. I found out, however, that empathy is not always generously distributed among those who are in or who wish to enter counseling as a profession.

A student revealed this fact to me several years after I began teaching counselor education. She was a young woman who was articulate, bright, and full of energy. She was wonderful in many ways. Yet, she could not demonstrate an ability to master empathy beyond an elementary level. I have no doubt she felt for her clients. The trouble was she could not convey it. In frustration, she usually ended up offering clients advice rather than letting them know that she felt with them. Finally, one day after a particularly tough supervision session, she confessed her inadequacy in the domain of empathy to me by saying,

"Feelings to me are just like music. When a song is over, I always play the next selection."

Her message spoke volumes (if not albums) about her ability and suitability for the counseling profession. She was kind and intelligent, but she lacked the patience to stay with a client and to deeply feel what the client might be experiencing.

We, as counselors, cannot truly be with or help others beyond the realm of giving them information unless we can empathize with them. That is a challenge and requires not only that we suspend judgment but also that we activate the right words within us like musicians playing the proper notes in a symphony. In such sound, there is connectivity that brings people together.

chapter 32

AFRAID OF BLOOD

She came to me is desperation. I knew she did not want to be there. Yet, there she was. Her intake form stated that she had a phobia. It was specific: blood.

I began our session by talking about phobias and the foundation for them. She was mildly interested but finally stopped me in midsentence and with some emotion said, "I've got to get over this fear fast."

"What's the rush?" I inquired.

"I want to go to medical school. A physician can't be afraid of blood."

She was right. Medicine of even the gentlest nature deals with blood. So, I suggested we center our sessions on Joseph Wolpe's systematic desensitization approach and go from there. She readily agreed once she understood the process, and within a few sessions she had gone through her hierarchy of most feared situations involving blood.

"What do I do next?" she asked.

"I don't think you have to do much more of anything, but if you wish you could view some movies that are of minor operations," I offered. She did and viewed some with major operations too.

Then her question came again: "What do I do next?"

"Nothing," I said. "I think you have done enough and you have completely overcome your problem."

However, she did not quit, and the last time I saw her she had just come back from a visit to a slaughterhouse.

Sometimes what is therapeutic can be taken to extremes. Knowing how far to take a process and when to stop is crucial. Preventive measures can be therapeutic but if overdone or taken to extremes can lead to disorders.

chapter | 33

OMELETS

A client theme I have heard constantly over the years is that of regret. "If only I had not said what I said or did what I did, everything would be so much better." Yet, people make mistakes and many times do not forgive themselves—let alone forget such incidents.

The importance of working in the "now" in such cases became apparent to me one day when I was seeing a man who was upset about the course of his life. He had had a bad relationship with his parents, he had chosen an inappropriate college and an esoteric major, he had married the wrong woman twice, and his career track had been as spotty as a leopard. So at the age of 56, he said,

"I want to go back and do it all over again."

"That would be nice," I replied, "but can you?"

He sighed and looked down at the ground. I could read his disappointment in my response. I did not want him to be unrealistic about his life as it was now. However, I did not want him to become hopelessly depressed over the state of his existence either. So I said, knowing a little about his personal habits, "Paul, what do you usually have for breakfast?"

"Why, a fried egg," he said.

"And if you make a mistake in breaking the egg, what do you do?"

"Well, either I break another and make an omelet or I scramble the egg."

"But you don't try to put the egg back in its casing?"

He laughed. "That would be impossible."

And then he caught the implication of what he knew to be true. He could not undo what had been done, but he could take the mess that lay before him and try to make the most of it by learning from it and forming it into something that was more palatable physically and mentally than what he had now.

People cannot unscramble eggs or undo events. But making the most out of what has been rather than trying to do the impossible can make a big difference in how one grows and lives.

Points to ponder |

1. What changes have you made in life that were memorable? Do you think small or big changes are easiest to implement? Why?

2. What behaviors have you or those you know well modeled? What were the results?

3. Find examples of people who failed in their lives and later became successful. Try to find factors that account for these turnarounds.

Section | five

MULTICULTURAL AND SPIRITUAL CONSIDERATIONS

With age she has learned
to forgive the groups
that mistreated her
because of her color.
Each Saturday she now bakes bread
and takes it to the local mission
where she stays to cut and serve it
with love and a main dish.
Her grace has overcome years of hatred,
angry words, and hours of sadness.
Her brightness exudes a subtle warmth.
Everyone calls her "Rainbow."

—*Gladding, 1999*[3]

The earth is not only constantly in motion but also changing. The heroes of yesterday are not the same as today. The mixture of the population differs too. In the United States, for instance, people of color are quietly becoming a majority. This type of change gives us pause because we sometimes hang onto the past in the hope that it will become the future. Yet, the only secure knowledge we have is that change is inevitable and sometimes it accelerates to become something we never expected. That is why being sensitive to other cultures outside of one's own is crucial to being an effective counselor.

The stories in this section emphasize the appreciation of life beyond limited cultural boundaries. What we do in regard to this phenomenon has implications for both how we counsel and how we live. Ask yourself as you read, what experiences have you had outside of your level of cultural comfort, and how have they affected you?

chapter | 34

AN ENCOUNTER WITH THE KLAN

I can still remember hearing the car horns in the distance. They were coming. The Ku Klux Klan was holding a rally on the courthouse square of my hometown of Decatur, Georgia, and they were driving up Church Street in front of my house as a part of their route. I was 10 years old, and up to that point my family had tried to protect me as much as possible from the sounds and the sights of the divided society that was the South of the 1950s. That summer day was no exception as my father quickly shooed me inside. Innocence was about to be lost, and he knew it. Yet, he tried as best he could to keep my brother, my sister, and me as far removed as possible from the evil that was to pass before us.

In retrospect I am sure he thought of sending us away for the day. However, he probably knew that such a tactic would backfire later. There was no escape from the pervasiveness of racism that dominated southern culture at the time. It was simply accepted and legally codified. Blacks and Whites were different races that should be kept separate and segregated from each other because Blacks were perceived as inferior. That view covered everything in its day like kudzu and strangled out reasonable discussions and change. So, as the car horns became louder and the Klan caravan drew closer, I was confined to the screened-in front porch of our house to watch silently a noisy parade full of people in hoods, Confederate battle flags, and the screaming of words that were offensive. The instructions from my father were clear: "You may look," he told me, "but you must remain as still as the humid air."

My wait was not long in coming, but while I sat, I thought as well as anticipated. I had read about the Klan and its origin. I knew that Nathan Bedford Forrester had founded the Klan in Tennessee after the Civil War to suppress the freedom of Blacks and keep them fearful and subservient to Whites. I had read of a recent Klan rally and cross burning at nearby Stone Mountain on a Saturday night in the Sunday edition of *The Atlanta Journal and Constitution* that I helped my brother deliver. I was not as naive as my father thought or wished. Yet, I did not know anyone who was an affiliate or advocate for the Klan or its causes. That made sense because the group was one surrounded by secrecy. You became a target of its wrath only if you spoke out against what it tried to enforce by intimidation and murder. So, I sat quietly and watched as the first cars came by. I was to see what I had read about up close and face-to-face.

However, what happened was different from what I had envisioned. The distance from our porch to the street was about 50 feet, so I had a clear view. What surprised me was what I saw. Before me were people in vehicles who were faceless in the sense that I could not see who they were. It was like Halloween in the summertime. Over their heads were white sheets shaped in the form of hoods that prevented anyone from identifying them. Instead, from the holes in their masks I caught glimpses of faces—eyes, noses, and mouths—but nothing distinctive. Even more striking was the fact that as these people passed our house, they not only blew their horns but also waved. I was confused. I thought evil should look and act like evil. Here before me was the personification of prejudice waving enthusiastically and in a friendly manner. Something was disturbingly wrong with the picture. However, I did as instructed. I did not move a muscle for fear that my father would punish me. The whole parade lasted only about five minutes. Then the honking of car horns and the white-robed, faceless people disappeared from my immediate senses as they became lodged in my memory.

In reflecting on this one moment in time, I realize that that day and my internal reaction to the events before me have continued to have an impact on my life both personally and professionally. For one thing, I saw then, and see even more clearly now, that racism is often faceless and parades around as if it were something else. The camouflage of racism and its pretentious nature makes it elusive and difficult to get a handle on—let alone address constructively.

chapter | 35

SHIRLEY

She was an older woman seated in the middle of my Monday night class on introduction to counseling. She stood out in both her manner and looks—well-dressed and gray-haired in the midst of blue jeans and youth. I glanced at her, smiled, and thought to myself, "She doesn't have a prayer."

It wasn't that I knew this woman. It was that I had known other older women. I had had them in my classes before in North Carolina and in Connecticut. I knew they had to be the same in Alabama. These women were usually not my best students. In fact, I could easily think of half a dozen examples of older women who had gotten my past classes offtrack by making comments related to anything but the materials we were studying. I could also think of many tests on which these women had not been clear, concise, or articulate about counseling.

Now please understand, I had a great love for my Grandmother Templeman, a woman whom we had called "Pal" as children and who was sharp mentally until her death at age 87. I also appreciated and admired the kindness of other older women I had encountered in church and in civic life. It seems they were always generous to a fault with mint candies in their purses and with nurturing words. These were strong women who combined goodness with kindness. Yet, give me an older woman in class, and I cringed because of my past experiences. The combination seemed to be like poetry and power tools. They just did not seem to go together.

But instead of fantasizing about how this older woman would do, I decided to face my bias and find out something about her as the rest of the class arrived. I introduced myself and then said, "Who are you?"

"My name is Shirley Ratliff," she replied, without volunteering any other information.

"Welcome to the class," I said, and then in a more direct way than is usually my manner (and that must have reflected prejudice), I queried, "Why are you here?"

"I want to learn how to be a counselor" was her straightforward answer. "I've been volunteering at sites that require counseling skills. I want to learn how to do things right and be a professional."

"If you work hard, you will learn," I assured her, wanting to believe my own words and transcend obvious doubts. Thus ended my first conversation with Shirley, a person to whom I would later dedicate a book.

So why do I tell you this story? The answer I think is because Shirley was the antithesis of all my preconceived ideas. She was bright, witty, articulate, and thoughtful. To this day I consider her to be the epitome of what a counseling student should be. If it had not been for Shirley, my life experience would be much poorer. Worse yet, I would still harbor a bias against the potency of older women.

chapter | 36

WASPs

I can still hear her opening words as we sat down in the corner office overlooking the parking lot.

"I don't like WASPs!" she said emphatically.

She was African American, and here I was as White an Anglo-Saxon Protestant as they came. In addition, I was male, which I am sure was not a factor in my favor.

"Didn't anybody screen this client?" I thought. "Why was she given to me? What am I going to do now?"

"I don't like WASPs," she repeated as forcefully as her first statement. (I did not need to be reminded, but she continued.) "They are awful! They get in your face. They get in your hair. I don't know why the Good Lord made them."

"I don't think I am being affirmed here," I said silently to myself. "There are some real feelings coming from this client, and I have yet to utter a word."

However, since the subject had come up, I asked her, "Tell me more about WASPs and your dislike for them."

She stared at me in disbelief, as if to say, "What am I not conveying about my disdain for WASPs?" However, after a brief pause she said, looking up, "As a little girl I was stung a number of times by them. Our house, like your office, had lots of them in it."

Her words and her look caught my attention. She was not talking about a group of people. She was talking about insects, and as I looked at the windows, which she could see more clearly than me, I realized fully the reason she had begun our session as she had. There must have been at least a half dozen wasps behind the blinds. It did not take 20/20 vision to see them outlined by the sun, flying in short bursts.

I immediately called downstairs to find a new room for counseling and to alert the secretary that we needed to call a pest control company. As we sat down in our new quarters I also confessed my thoughts to the woman in front of me. She was kind in her remarks, although she quickly revealed that she had suffered insults, discrimination, and indignation from White, Protestant men in her life and wondered why she had been matched up with me. I offered to find her someone new, but after addressing the issue, she wanted to go ahead with the session. We did, and her difficulty, which focused on a child, was a matter that was eventually resolved.

However, what sticks in my mind to this day is the fact that if the office I chose to work in had not had insects in the windows, I might be less sensitive now to cultures and to how my own background heritage influences what I do in counseling sessions. WASPs and wasps can be beneficial. However, they can also be frightening and dangerous. Who we are and how we look affects others on multiple levels.

chapter | 37

SPIRITS, SPIRITUALITY, AND COUNSELING

I had only one item with me that day in the grocery store line. It was a bottle of wine. I was going to a newly married couple's home, and I wanted to take them a present. I was pleased that I had remembered to stop and get them a gift. What I did not notice was that I had forgotten to take off my nametag from work. I was doing a clinical internship in the chaplain's department at a local hospital. It was an exciting opportunity, and I was learning a lot about counseling and spirituality. However, when I presented the bottle of wine to the cashier, she looked at me disapprovingly after reading my nametag. When I realized what was happening, I tried to make light of the whole situation.

"Would you believe this wine is for communion?" I inquired.

"When did white wine start making it to the altar?" she countered.

"How about medicinal purposes?"

"What ails you?" she retorted. "We have a complete pharmacy department in this store."

"Actually, this wine is for a newly married couple," I confessed.

"They don't need it," was all she could say. "Save it for when they get old and aren't so peppy."

Well, I bought the wine, received my change, and hurried out the door slightly embarrassed, wishing I had the bag she had put the bottle in over my head instead.

Spirituality and counseling is not a story about wine or presents. Rather, it is an emphasis within the profession on helping people become more aware of their spiritual side as a part of their lives. That process is easier for some to check out than for others, but it is a vital dimension of counseling, whether one works in a chaplain's department or in a more secular setting.

chapter | 38

PUTTING ON THE GLOVES WITH MOTHER TERESA

In December 1995 I took a group of students to Calcutta, India, to work in the homes of Mother Teresa. It was a moving and uplifting experience, spiritual in the best sense of that word as our small band mixed daily with Muslims, Hindus, Christians, and others who lived and worked in the places where we volunteered. Along the way I had the privilege of actually meeting Mother Teresa who both looked like her pictures (small, frail, stooped, and wrinkled) and lived up to her reputation. She literally broke off conversation with me and our group to go clean toilets.

However, what I remember most about my three weeks in the City of Joy was the work I did in the homes, especially the daily bathing of sick and infirmed men at Prem Dan, a home for those who are too physically and mentally disabled to take care of themselves. The men were just getting ready for their baths when I arrived each morning. Many were in wheelchairs, some were on crutches, and a number were mobile but a bit shaky on their feet.

The only hot water for bathing was boiled over a stove in large kettles. There was never enough of it, and cold water rinses and sometimes full baths were mostly the norm. The most labor-intensive part of the bathing process, though, was getting the night clothes off of the men and scrubbing down those too infirmed to do so for themselves. On numerous occasions, I not only removed clothing but also scraped dried feces from these men's buttocks and legs. That job was never pleasant but was always necessary. To be safe, I wore latex gloves and would say to myself as the work began, "I'm putting on the gloves with Mother Teresa" (who I knew from my previous experience used gloves at times, too).

Other interactions with the men included shaving their heads as a preventive way of dealing with lice and shaving their faces so they would feel cleaner and more refreshed. Both jobs were done with razors that were anything but new and sharp. It was a grueling task and yet one I loved because the men seemed so appreciative even when I cut them (which unfortunately was often).

As I reflected then and now about my time in Calcutta, I think of how different and similar the work there was to the counseling I have done. The behavior of care was expressed physically and mostly nonverbally in India, whereas in the United States I have been mostly cognitive and verbal in what I have given to others. I could see my results immediately at Prem Dan, whereas in counseling I seldom see such tangible evidence. Yet, in both cases, I knew that what I did made a real difference. I also realized anew that helping is not one-dimensional.

I was blessed to enter the lives of some downtrodden men in the middle of the last decade of the 20th century. They taught me gratitude for the circumstances of my own life but more importantly helped me see and feel life more fully. Calcutta embodied the worst of human life, yet paradoxically it brought out the best within me and others who shared the experience. What a surprise!

chapter | 39

GETTING THERE

Knowledge is important in our society because it helps inform and direct. Without knowledge, we misunderstand and are misunderstood. This fact became personalized in my life one June day in Calais, France. It was before the opening of the English/French tunnel, and I was waiting with a friend to catch a boat back to Dover. It was hot, and to pass the time we read whatever we could find. All of a sudden, my friend became excited as he pointed to a sign.

"Look," he said. "We are going to have problems. We are taking a boat to Britain with people who are mentally and physically limited."

I glanced up to read the words announcing this phenomenon for myself. Sure enough, on the schedule chart was the name of our boat, and out by the side of it was the word "retarded," that is, delayed. Knowing just a bit of French I was able to tell my friend that he should be more worried about his inability to understand a foreign language than the type of passengers onboard our ship.

Getting somewhere in counseling is based on knowledge. However, sometimes because of unforeseen events we may be delayed in acquiring information as rapidly as would be ideal. At such times, we may become frustrated because of the delay. If we know that fact before departing into the uncharted waters of change and clients, we will be calmer, and the process will go more smoothly, even if it is slower.

Points to ponder |

1. What experiences do you have with people outside your immediate cultural group(s)? What opinions do you have of these people? Why?

2. Age discrimination is illegal but still occurs. Project your life 10 years from now. How would you like to be seen and treated?

3. Prejudice is usually subtle. Where have you seen prejudice in your environment, and how have you seen it effectively dealt with?

Section | six

THE INFLUENCES OF COLLEAGUES, FRIENDS, AND FAMILY

I walk thoughtfully down Beecher Road
at the end of a summer of too little growth,
the autumn wind stirring around me,
orange remnants of once green leaves.
I am the son of a fourth-grade teacher
and a man who dabbled in business and roses,
a descendant of Virginia farmers
and open-minded Baptists,
the husband of a Connecticut woman,
the father of growing children.
Youngest of three, I am a trinity
counselor
teacher
writer.
Amid the cold, I approach home,
midlife is full of surprises.

—Gladding, 1998[4]

The influence of family, friends, and colleagues cannot be overestimated. These are the people whom we are closest to and most dependent on in life. They are the ones who are there for us when we are under stress and who rejoice with us when there are events to celebrate. These individuals listen to us, empathize with us, and know us best. If they are healthy and wise, we become better because of the association. If they are too absorbed in their own affairs, we and our relationships with them may suffer.

The stories in this section are focused on events connected collectively with this group of people. As you read these vignettes try to remember times in your life when your family, friends, and colleagues have made a positive impact on what you did, thought, or felt or how you perceived a situation. What did they do? What did you learn and take away from the experience(s)?

chapter | 40

THE OFFICE

The first office I had as a clinician was in a room with two other people, a rehabilitation counselor and a substance abuse counselor. Each of us had a desk, a chair, and a lamp. The first one to arrive each morning turned on the overhead light, and the last one to leave at night flicked it off. When we had clients, the other two colleagues left. I thus learned to be adaptable quite early in my career and to conduct counseling sessions while sitting on stairs in a hallway or walking around a parking lot. However, I enjoyed working in the office. I always felt fortunate when my roommates either left it to me or were somewhere else. The office made me feel more professional.

Yet, I found out from this experience that offices are not as valuable as colleagues. There were numerous times when I consulted with each of them for information or strategies to use with my clients. They were gracious to a fault although they had their own peculiarities, such as the substance abuse counselor not being able to go for long periods of time without having a cup of coffee.

Since that early experience, I have been less impressed with my surroundings than with the people with whom I work. A desk, a chair, a lamp, and four walls are easy to replace. A sensitive and smart colleague is priceless, especially one who provides you with support and insight.

chapter | 41

HAPPENSTANCE: NOTE WHOM YOU QUOTE

A presentation I made in 1979 was before the Division of Humanistic Psychology in New York City. At that time I had become intrigued, because of my clinical experiences, with the use of the arts in counseling, especially the use of poetry. Therefore, my presentation was on the use of poetry as therapy in counseling. I had abundant case examples, but I needed to have a better knowledge of the underlying theory on which my work was based. Fortunately for me, a book entitled *Poetry as Therapy* (Lerner, 1978) arrived about two months before my presentation, and I had time to read it thoroughly and digest its contents before the convention. It was a jewel of a book, and I remember how grateful I was for its timely publication.

Thus on a sunny September morning, I stood up to address about 25 people in a hotel suite at the Waldorf Astoria on a subject that I had an interest in and now had some background material on. As I began my remarks I told my audience how my clients often brought in or wrote poems during their counseling sessions and how I had found these poems to offer catharsis, insight, and relief. I then said that in addition to what I intuitively knew about the value of poetry, I had recently read a book on its uses in therapy.

"The author/editor of the book is a guy named Arthur Lerner from Los Angeles," I stated. "I don't know him. Does anybody?"

"I'm Lerner," piped up a balding older gentleman in the front row.

"You are?" I gulped. "Arthur Lerner, the author/editor of *Poetry as Therapy*?"

"The same," he responded.

"I hope I'm quoting you correctly," I replied.

"Go on," he gently commanded. And I did.

After the presentation, I received a number of immediate comments about what had been discussed, but none were from Arthur Lerner. Instead, he came up to me and asked, "What are you doing for dinner tonight?"

I was free, and so about 6 p.m. I found myself in his company, along with that of his wife, Matilda. We talked for several hours, and I received much food for thought as well as substance. The next week Art called me. We again discussed the use of poetry in the therapeutic process. Later he invited me out to California to do a workshop at UCLA, and a few years afterward I wrote a chapter for him in a book he edited on the uses of literature in the therapeutic experience. Until his death in 1997, Art was a close friend although we lived 3,000 miles apart. He introduced me to a larger world of counseling that I would never have been exposed to had he not befriended and mentored me.

I had no way of knowing that I would meet Arthur Lerner or that I would benefit so much from him. I think that is the way it is with counseling sometimes too. People and words come to us, and in them and through them we are enriched as well as enrich others. There is no way of knowing when such times will come. It is all a delightful surprise of being a continuous learner.

chapter | 42

SOURCES WITHIN

One event in my life that created a crisis equal to those I have faced with many clients was a broken engagement. I was in my 20s at the time and had limited knowledge and skill. It was an event I wish had never happened because of the pain I went through. Yet, in retrospect what I learned from the breakup probably changed the course of my life for the better. As with anyone who has gone through the dissolving of an intimate relationship, I was not immune to the turmoil of conflictual feelings that tossed about and numbed my mind as well as penetrated through the very fiber of my body and into my bones. Termination came, and reality sank in. Depression became a constant companion. I was not near family or friends. Rather, I was isolated. In my initial attempts to get past the situation, I found myself talking to those who I knew around me. However, reaching out on my part did not produce anything positive.

"So what do I do now?" I thought. There was no clear answer or direction. No signal, sign, or inspiration came. Thus, I waited, feeling fatigued, discouraged, hopeless, and abandoned. In the midst of this time, one night I went to sleep and really wondered what I would do the next day if things were not better. That night I had a dream like none I have had before or since. In the dream I saw myself in a desert. I could feel the hot sand beneath me, see the bleak landscape before me, and even feel a dryness in my throat. I actually felt myself crawling along. I remember wondering, "Will I live through this experience?"

At a point where I put my head down in the sand and was about to give up, a strange thing happened. Out of nowhere, four of my ancestors appeared on the scene. I did not know but one of them personally, my Grandmother Templeman who had died a few years before. However, I recognized all of the people from my family's historical past by name and face, for I had seen their pictures in frames in our house and heard stories about them that had been told to me as a child. I did not move, but I remember my grandmother saying, "You're exhausted. We'll carry you until you're able to walk again." And with that, they lifted me up.

From that moment on I knew I would make it through the trauma I was facing and that my life would eventually be okay. I also knew I would get through the pain of the crisis I was in and that regardless of what events happened in the future, I would get through them as well. I have. It is not that life has been easy. It has not. But I know that from struggle and pain, inner resources can come into play and outer resources can be tapped so that in the midst of angst, anxiety, or despondency, we can become different in a better—not a bitter—way.

chapter | 43

COOL UNDER FIRE

My work as a counselor has sometimes taken me on the road. In such cases, I have often timed my out-of-the-office experiences to coincide with an opportunity to have lunch with someone. On one such occasion I met a rehabilitation counselor who was a good friend.

As we sat eating our blue-plate specials of barbecue in a greasy restaurant, we discussed different aspects of being a counselor. The conversation included a wide range of topics from diagnosis to burnout. We were intensely involved in our discussion in the back of the seating area away from others and were engrossed in our own little world. Thus, we were annoyed at the close, loud sound of sirens from the outside. However, they stopped, and we continued with our dialogue, which was at times a bit hot and heavy.

Finally, I got up to get some water because no waitress had come by in a while. As I left our area I found more than I was looking for. Several firemen were entering the building with hoses. (I knew they could spare some water, but I did not ask.)

During our conversation a small kitchen fire had started. We had been overlooked by the management and, uninformed, had continued to interact as if nothing was happening while in actuality a part of the roof had burned.

An hour or so later when I was back at the office, I joked with the rehabilitation counselor about keeping our cool under fire. At the same time I realized that, joking aside, it is what you do not know that can harm you.

chapter | 44

SCARS

I heard the shrill cry. It was ear piercing, the kind of sound a badly hurt animal might make. "Why don't people take better care of their children," I thought. It is quite annoying to have to put up with this kind of noise when on vacation and browsing at a beach souvenir shop.

Yet, hardly had I formulated the sentence when I knew something was terribly wrong. My wife, Claire, was calling my name as she came running from the back of the shop to the front. In her arms was our then four-year-old, Timothy, bleeding badly and screaming at the top of his lungs.

"Here," she said, handing our son off to me like a football. "Try to stop the bleeding. I'll call for help."

Even though I had been in the Army, the sight of Timothy gave me pause. He had stumbled face first with his mouth open onto the outstretched metal arm of a coat rack. The force of gravity had carried him down, and as he fell, the long appendage that he had fallen on had penetrated his cheek and torn a large gash in the right side of his mouth from the inside out. A woman handed me a towel. I knew to apply pressure both to stop the bleeding and to cover up the sight of a shocking wound.

When help did not arrive soon, we hustled Timothy, our other two sons, and ourselves into what instantly became our Dodge Care-A-Van and headed for the emergency room of the nearest hospital in Myrtle Beach, South Carolina. There Timothy and I spent two hours with a plastic surgeon while everyone else waited anxiously. The rest of the summer and early fall were spent in attending to the healing process, which was gradual with less than desired results. Therefore, Timothy underwent more procedures until over a year later the scar he had as a result of the accident, although noticeable, was not his most prominent feature.

The trauma and the recovery process I observed and felt as Timothy's father are parallel to events in some of our clients' lives. Usually clients come in with psychological rather than physical scars. Yet, the trauma and pain associated with the events that have propelled them to our offices are as real as metal coat racks.

They have fallen in some way and been hurt. Recovery takes time and can be frustrating. There are a number of anxious moments. Even when the helping process ends, a residue of unpleasant memories may linger although more muted or faded. If we and our clients do our work well, these scars will not be the most noticed or noteworthy feature of their lives.

chapter | 45

COURTLAND, THE TURKEYS, AND ME IN KNOXVILLE, TENNESSEE

One of the joys of being in counseling is serving the profession as an associational officer. I have done this several times, but at no time has it been any more fun than when I was president of the Association for Counselor Education and Supervision the same year that Dr. Courtland Lee was president of the American Counseling Association. Part of the reason may have to do with contrast. I am a petite (5' 3") White man with a wiry build, whereas Courtland is a tall (6' 3") African American man with a slender build. When we are together, we look like polar opposites, and people tend to stare at us.

As it happened one November afternoon, we both gave brief speeches to the Southern Association for Counselor Education and Supervision in Knoxville, Tennessee. To show gratitude for what we had done, the officers of the association presented each of us with a papier-mâché turkey. The birds were beautifully decorated but were quite large (about the size of basketballs, or "butterballs" in turkey language). Fortunately, they had a wire handle on their bodies by which to carry them, and that made getting them up to our hotel rooms easier. On the way up to the rooms in the elevator, Courtland and I discovered we had the same flight the next day so we decided to catch a taxi together.

Sunday morning came, and we both arrived at the lobby at the same time carrying our bags and turkeys. We hailed a cab and put our suitcases in the trunk while we placed the turkeys in our laps. It was in reaching the airport that the fun really began. Here we were, a short White man and a tall Black man carrying identical papier-mâché turkeys through the lobby of the airport and up to the ticket counter. The personnel behind the desk just smiled, checked our luggage, and told us that if we wanted to keep our turkeys in one piece we would have to carry them on the plane. They also told us our flight was located at the farthest gate from the ticket counter.

So we proceeded to walk together holding our turkeys as they bobbed along on their wire hangers. I felt at times as if we were on a platform stage in Atlantic City like they have for the Miss America contest, and that people were watching us both intensely and in disbelief. Regardless, I think we brought some real humor to those we passed. I know the memory of our turkey walk continues to this day as does our friendship. Counseling is inclusive. It encompasses a variety of people (and sometimes birds of a different feather) who interact, learn, and have good times together.

Points to ponder |

1. What have you learned from good colleagues and friends that continues to be of value to you?

2. What have you learned about yourself in times of failure or despair? How do you use that knowledge now?

3. How have chance encounters influenced your development or friendships? Be specific.

Section | seven

WORKING WITH GROUPS AND FAMILIES

Emotions ricochet around the group
fired by an act of self-disclosure
in an atmosphere of trust.
I, struck by the process,
watch as feelings penetrate the minds
of involved members
and touch off new reactions.
Change comes from many directions
triggered by simple words.
—*Gladding, 1999*[5]

Some of the most trying and rewarding experiences we can have in counseling come when we do therapeutic work with groups and families. The dynamics differ dramatically in these situations as opposed to those when counseling is delivered on a one-to-one basis. Working with groups and families can be a bit bizarre and/or humorous, such as in this section's vignettes on "Sex Therapy: The Challenge" and "Humor." Likewise, experiences with these populations can be dramatic and enlightening, such as in the stories here on "Three's a Crowd but Four's a Family Counseling Session" and "Drama Break."

Regardless of the immediate impact, it is crucial that we as counselors work with groups and families. Not only is such an arrangement more economical for clients, but it may be more significant in the long run because few clients live outside the influence of these groups in their everyday lives.

chapter | 46

THE OTHER SIDE OF LABELS

One of my most memorable experiences as a counselor was in working with a schizophrenic man in a group. I was relatively new to the counseling profession and inexperienced at running groups. The man was a veteran of mental health services and had gone through a number of psychiatrists, psychologists, counselors, social workers, and nurses before he got to me. Like a tidal wave on a beach, he was pretty overwhelming, and I was not sure what to do with him. I sensed he did not expect a moment's trouble from me. A few words, a little action, and I too would probably give up on him. He would "win," having defeated another clinician again.

However, I did not do what he expected because I really did not know how. I kept treating him with respect; I did not follow him out of the room when he would get upset in the group. I always thanked him for his input. One day he could not stand it any longer. He said to me, "Where did you go to school, and did you really learn anything about mental health services there?" Before I could reply, he went on with a statement: "You don't know how to work with schizophrenics. Listen, I'm schizophrenic. Everybody tells me that, and I've tried to show you. You're never going to make it in this profession unless you learn to become agitated instead of treating me like a normal person."

"Oh," I replied. "Wouldn't it be easier if you tried something new? I mean I'm not a quick study, and there must be something you wish to do besides what you're doing."

He looked puzzled, but he stayed in the group that day. To my surprise, as the group went on, he began telling the other members about some land he had seen near his family's farm that he would like to work. One thing led to another and his hope turned into plans and finally action as he began to make a transition.

The point is that through discussing who he was in the group he discovered another side of himself that was healthier than he expected. That self was able to grow in the "we-ness" that was the group. As far as I know, he is still on the land he purchased and a part of a productive community.

chapter | 47

THE POWER OF NANCY DREW

The power of literature struck me a few years ago when I was working with a group of adolescents. In the group was a young woman who wanted to be recognized for her independence and ability. As the group went on I asked her,

"Whom do you know who is like you want to be?"

To my surprise she said, "Nancy Drew."

"Oh," I replied. "What is it about Miss Drew that makes her attractive to you?"

To which she stated, "Nancy can think for herself. She is courageous, and she is just as smart and able as any boy."

From then on when the young woman would talk about what she wished to achieve, a group member would always ask, "How would Nancy Drew do it?"

"Like this," the young woman would reply as she enacted positive behaviors before all assembled.

chapter | 48

AIRTIME

Everyone needs air in order to survive. Participants in a group need air in order to thrive. Let me explain.

By "air" in a group I am not referring to the gaseous mixture of elements surrounding the earth that all of us breathe. Rather, I am referring to the amount of time a person gets to speak in a group. Group members learn from each other both directly and vicariously. In order to learn best, however, they need to have time to give a voice to what they have processed externally and internally. Some need more time to "air" than others, but everyone needs to be heard.

Even in groups that are primarily task or educationally related, members do best when they are empowered to speak and when they realize their voice is valued. In such cases, they take "ownership" of the group and contribute more to it.

By obtaining input at the beginning of each group, for example through "go-rounds" (where every member gets a chance to talk), the group progresses. It is like one member told me after I solicited information from him:

"When I speak I feel as if I'm not just another person who fills a chair. I think when you and others ask me for an opinion, you really care. That makes me feel alive."

chapter | 49

THREE'S A CROWD BUT FOUR'S A FAMILY COUNSELING SESSION

For some families that come to counseling, there is a lack of trying by family members, and the result is a trying experience. A vivid memory I have of resistance to change came when I once saw a family that was supposed to be composed of four people. As I greeted the family, I noticed only three people.

"I'm a bit confused," I said. "I see that you report that you are a family of four, but I count only three noses. Since I assume there is a nose connected with each person, it appears to me that we are a person short."

"That would be Eleanor," said the mother. "We call her the 'Wild Thing.' She's in the car but refuses to come in."

"How big is Eleanor?" I asked.

"About 98 pounds," said the father. "She's 13 years old."

"Well," I replied. "Go get Eleanor and bring her into the session. I am charging you, and the clock is running. We won't start the session without her."

The protests were great.

"She'll scratch our eyes out," said her brother.

"She'll never speak to us again," groaned the mother.

"She'll never let us come back," sighed the father.

"Go get her," I repeated.

Thus, they reluctantly went out to the parking lot. What occurred next was not a pretty sight. There was a bit of a struggle and a few raised voices, but with the odds at 3 to 1, about 10 minutes later Eleanor was brought into my office with her parents and brother carrying her like a captured wild animal.

I interacted with the family, including Eleanor, the rest of the session. We focused on how to tame the "wild thing" that was Eleanor, and in talking with her family, Eleanor actually offered some good suggestions. However, the important part of the therapeutic work started with a change in the family's interaction with their scapegoated daughter. The parents had taken some control over a situation about which they had previously felt helpless and angry. The bringing in of Eleanor brought the family into dealing with issues that were separating them. There was no magic to the process—only a struggle. However, there was change that years later resulted in visits, hugs, phone calls, and mail that kept the family together even with time and aging.

chapter | 50

SEX THERAPY: THE CHALLENGE

A young couple I once saw had two difficulties: They had sexual problems and were mentally challenged. I was not married and was somewhat reluctant to work with them because of this personal circumstance. However, my supervisor told me that he thought I was no more limited than the couple, so (taking that as a compliment) I agreed to work with them. In order to do the best job possible I thought it important to study sex manuals and be familiar with body parts and functions. Thus, I checked out a bevy of books and studied late for several evenings to my delight and edification.

Then I went into the session with great anatomical information and the intent to find out exactly what the problem was and resolve it.

"What brings you here?" I inquired.

"A 1986 Ford pickup" was the answer I received.

Undaunted, I then asked both people in my best clinical voice what was of most concern to them sexually. I received only vague and convoluted answers in regard to the specifics about which I was inquiring. Finally frustrated, I tried a concrete approach and said,

"Tell me this. Just how far have you two gone?" To that the young woman looked at her husband curiously and he at her. Then she looked at me and replied in a rather matter-of-fact manner, "Well, we've gone about as far as Atlanta."

From her response (which was much more literal than I wanted), I realized that competency and change are interrelated. If counseling is to be meaningful, a simple and unconfused language must be used. Furthermore, I found out that pertinent questions asked in the wrong way will get responses that are unbelievably off the mark.

chapter | 51

DRAMA BREAK

Sometimes people need a break in the way they relate to one another. Such a break creates opportunities. I first realized this fact while working with a dysfunctional couple. He was a construction worker, massive in size but slow in speech. She was a secretary, speedy in her clerical skills and fast with her opinions. The trouble was that when they would argue, she would begin to outtalk him. In frustration and anger, he would grab her arm and twist it around her back until she was quiet. (I used to call them the twist and shout couple after one of my favorite songs from the 1960s by the Righteous Brothers. However, there was nothing melodious about their relationship.)

One day they came in to see me, and the pattern started again. Just like Bob Dylan used to sing that you do not have to be a weatherman to know which way the wind is blowing, I realized that one need not be a family counselor to see the gathering storm of conflict emerging within a relationship. Thus, rather than wait for the thunder and lightning of what was to come, I asked the couple to freeze in their tracks as if a gust of cold arctic air had just swept over them. (This type of action was not too hard for any of us to imagine because each winter strong cold fronts frequently swept into the state of Connecticut in which we lived.)

After they froze in place, I told them we were going to act out a scene. The man was to play himself and express his concerns but speak in a slower than normal voice. The woman was to act just the opposite of her usual behavior. She was simply to listen. As she did, she was to pick up on his words as she might pick up on dictation, and she was to read his body cues in addition to understanding his language. Then she was to give her husband feedback about what she heard and saw. With that explained, I then shouted, "Action!"

They performed well and talked about the event at some length after I yelled, "Cut!" Then we reversed the roles. Although there was no camera or lights, insight and understanding emerged from these staged dramatic moments. Had we not stopped for some drama, the situation might have stayed the same or deteriorated.

However, a new sense of timing led to new understanding and more productive ways of interacting. Some weeks later, I actually saw the couple at a concert together looking as if they were really enjoying themselves as they danced to some upbeat music on the grass to the tune by which I had described them earlier: "Twist and Shout."

chapter | 52

AN UNEXPECTED RECONCILIATION: LAURA ASHLEY

Of all the couples I have ever seen in my professional career, this one initially seemed the "most hopeless." She came from a wealthy and sophisticated background. He called her "Laura Ashley" the name on her well-tailored clothes and accessories. He came from poverty and was crude in manner, dress, and speech. He loved to hunt, fish, and drink beer with the boys. She called him "Billy Bob." He went from one manual labor job to another and liked the freedom it afforded him.

I wondered how they had ever found each other—much less me. I could imagine the initial excitement and attraction they had for one another because of their differences. However, I could not imagine that they would have carried their relationship all the way to the altar, tied the knot, and had a child 2 years later. Now in their 10th year of marriage, they sat before me. She complained that he was "uninteresting" and "boorish." He said she was too concerned with the little and unimportant things of life like her looks. "Why do you shop at those expensive stores?" he inquired.

"If ever there was a match not meant to be this is probably it," I thought. Thus, I was not surprised that she called after the first session and canceled the second.

"There is no use talking about our marriage," she said. "The writing is on the wall, and it reads 'Go directly to court and divorce.'"

I did not argue with her and thought that like so many couples I had seen in marriage counseling, this one came too late to get help.

What did surprise me was a call from him.

"I want to see you," he said. "I want to save our relationship."

I could have brushed him off I think and have put up a strong argument for him not coming for counseling, but he seemed sincere, so I agreed. A few days later he showed up, and we began what was the start of a long-term therapeutic relationship. I was truly amazed that he came each week. He passionately talked about "Laura Ashley," but I thought it was futile. How could he do anything to win her back?

"Tigers don't change their stripes," I once said to him.

"This tiger does," he responded.

So, he did. He was committed. He went back to school, changed careers, started working out, began reading books from *The New York Times* best-seller list, and even found a church to attend. I do not think I have ever seen anyone work harder for anything in my life. He showed up promptly for each of our appointments, too, and threw himself into our sessions. Rather than demand, he invited Laura Ashley to give him another try. On the fifth request, she consented to see him, and after that I began seeing them together. They made it back as a couple to my surprise. As they were leaving my office for the last time, he turned around and said, "From now on, please call me William."

Sometimes we, as counselors, work hard to promote change. The best times are when our clients do.

chapter | 53

HUMOR

Counseling is never a joke, but it does require a sense of humor, and there is often levity in it. Clients laugh more as they get better. Life is not so grave and serious. There is a connection, a positive correlation, between having some laughter in one's life and being able to deal effectively with reality.

Paul Watzlawick has pointed out that some situations are "hopeless but not serious" as well as "serious but not hopeless." Humor comes into play in those situations in which clients come to counseling feeling hopeless, especially if their situation is not serious, that is, is easily solvable. For instance, I once saw a couple in which each person was upset over the behavior of the other to be either orderly or sloppy. Friction in their lives revolved around how they would keep their house. One wanted everything neat; the other wanted everything casual. The breakthrough in their relationship (as opposed to the breakup of it) came when they agreed they would maintain both kinds of rooms, for example, the living room was formal but the bedroom was bohemian. When they saw the folly of what they had been fighting about and how relatively simple it was to solve, they laughed.

Clients are sometimes like a math book, full of problems. But as counselors we need to be solution-focused. Along with other clinical skills in such a process, humor helps us move from the unsolvable to the possible. Humor assists us in keeping our sanity and humanity while our clients work out ways to live life more fully.

chapter | 54

RESEARCH AND A REFRAME WITHIN THE FAMILY

Sometimes we can get too caught up in our professional lives. That fact was brought home to me literally in my home by my wife. I came to her one day enthusiastic about some research I had recently read. The article that had caught my attention was on marital happiness. It stated that a couple's degree of happiness decreased with each child they had. Claire, my wife, who was pregnant at the time with our third child and feeling queasy and tired with two toddlers underfoot, seemed nonplussed by my remarks. She even appeared to become a little annoyed as I droned on with some excitement about what I had found. By the time I had finished expounding on the implications of the work I had absorbed, I could tell she did not want to hear any more. Thus, I went back to my office and further study.

A couple of months later, the blessed event we had waited for, Timothy, arrived. It was a chilly March night, but the cold had no impact on the delivery. However, the previous conversation Claire and I had had about marital happiness was not finished. In recovery, with our new son close by her side, she looked up at me from the bed and said,

"The honeymoon's not over. There are just more people on it."

Sure enough, she was right. Although more stressed than ever before, we have more fun than previously because of the way we now interact with our children and each other. Claire's reframe on the situation changed the perspective we had as a couple without cooling my enthusiasm to read the research. It gave us the best of both worlds.

chapter | 55

WORDS ALONE

If you pay attention to words alone, you may find yourself alone and lonely, having failed to make an intervention that would be helpful. For instance, in working with a couple that had been a cantankerous duo together longer than I had been alive, whom I shall call the Bickersons, I realized I was doomed if I stayed with their verbal content. From the minute the couple arrived, they were at each other verbally. In fact, they were quite good at their word attacks. She would hit him with a barb, and he would jab back with an insult. Then she would land a demeaning comment squarely on his chin, and he would stagger but counterpunch with a discounting statement of his own. Back and forth, they went at it for about five minutes, flipping words as if they were flapjacks, until having demonstrated their potency, they stopped and turned to me, and the husband said (almost smugly, as if flipping me a hot one off the grill),

"So what are you going to do to help us?"

My blood was flowing like warm maple syrup, and my mind was racing in time with the words that had been let loose. I realized that instead of interacting in their arena I needed to change the scene if I was to avoid being fried, grilled, or burned. So, I replied,

"I'm sending you to your corners. That's the end of Round 1."

Thus, before you could say "Mohammed Ali," I got them on their feet and directed each to go to a separate corner of the office as if they were in a boxing ring and not cooking in the kitchen. Then I clapped my hands together and said, "Come out and sit down; it's Round 2." They did but were somewhat stunned. They had entered a new domain and a new way of seeing and being. In their new environment, well-worn ways of interacting were not allowed. New and productive ways of trying to relate were taught, tried, and modified. Everyone won.

Points to ponder |

1. Who are some people, either fictional or real, after whom you model your life? What characteristics do they have that you would like to emulate?

2. When did someone make a change you did not expect? How did that make you feel? What was the outcome of the change?

3. What do you find humorous? Think about a funny event in your family or a group and what made it so.

Section | eight

PROFESSIONAL DEVELOPMENT

I remember doing role plays in your class
trying to look cool, while my palms sweated
and my heart beat as fast as a hummingbird's wings.
You were supportive ... giving me feedback
while encouraging me to explore
the universe that was myself.
Other classes, other seasons came as quickly
as the sound of laughter and as silently as sorrow.
With you I traveled the roads to conventions
sharing all the light and darkness of the time that came to be.

—*Gladding, 1989*[6]

As professional counselors we either develop or stagnate. The half-life of knowledge is decreasing yearly, and the counselor who does not actively keep up will by default fall behind and become obsolete. Continuing education and supervision are two important ways of combating irrelevance and obsolescence.

The vignettes in this section highlight that fact along with the importance of counselors learning how the legal system works in regard to clients. Research and learning from others are also stressed. Planned movement in a growth-producing direction does not always meet with success, but it usually results in knowledge that is enabling.

chapter | 56

SUPERVISION

Supervision is a multidimensional process that helps counselors keep their skills current and potent. It is a learning experience that is essential for both novice and experienced clinicians.

When I initially became a counselor, I opted for supervision that was more didactic and instructive. However, over the years I have come to value and use peer supervision more. In such an atmosphere, growth occurs through input of fellow counselors and dialogue with them.

For instance, I remember being stuck as to some ways I could communicate the importance of a couple getting help for their daughter. A direct, rational approach had not worked. Then one of my fellow supervisors asked, "How do your clients get to your office?"

"There are many ways for them to get there," I replied.

"What does that tell you about your predicament?" was his response.

Indeed, the more I thought about it, the more I realized I could open up avenues for my clients to travel by having the couple "look down the road" of the options they had for their daughter. In the next session, I opened up with the road metaphor and instead of suggesting, I let my clients tell and sell me some possibilities for obtaining assistance. They found some options that were realistic and pragmatic. They even followed through on a couple of their better ideas and literally got somewhere. As a result, they were happier, I was less stressed, and the counseling was successful.

Supervision improves our abilities to see and be with our clients and to improve our clinical skills. It is a powerful way to overcome resistance that sometimes inadvertently is our own.

chapter | 57

COURT: THE RULES OF THE GAME

The first time I went to court as a counselor I went with a hope and a prayer. I should have gone prepared.

I assumed that a court of law was a place where all you had to do was "tell the truth, the whole truth, so help you God" and all would work out well. I was unaware of the rules of the games that attorneys play.

For instance, my attorney approached me like a warm teddy bear and pitched questions to me that could only be characterized as "softballs." "What was my name?" "What were my degrees?" "How had I handled the client in question?" When the questions were over, I felt like I had hit home runs every time I had come up to bat.

In contrast, the opposing attorney rushed toward me with all the characteristics of a grizzly bear. He bore down with queries that were a mixture of fastballs, curves, and sliders. The game had changed. We were playing "hardball." "Was my clinical degree from a nationally ranked program?" "What percentage of counselors would have done exactly what I did in regard to the client?" "Did I feel any sexual attraction to the client?" (That one my attorney objected to, as did I.) The long and short of what happened, however, was that after the cross-examination was over, I understood the Spanish Inquisition much better. I also knew what it was to "strike out" . . . repeatedly.

I have not been to court a lot since that first encounter. However, I have never gone without consulting an attorney and colleagues beforehand. The rules of the game are different, and to enter without an understanding is to invite a mauling.

chapter | 58

RESEARCH AND THEORY: A REMINDER FROM CARL

When I began my career, many of the pioneers of counseling were at their zenith. Therefore, I listened to lectures by Carl Rogers, Gilbert Wrenn, Albert Ellis, B. F. Skinner, Virginia Satir, and Carl Whitaker, among others. I even took a four-week course at the New School in New York City with Rollo May. Because I received a lot of firsthand information from these individuals, I thought I was in a position to critique their work or at least compare and contrast their approaches. I did so in the classes I was teaching. Then one day I thought I would put onc of my lectures in the form of an article and send it off for publication. I wrote a comparison between Heinz Kohut and Carl Rogers. It was published in the *Journal of Counseling and Development* in 1986. I felt good and proudly showed this pithy but what I considered profound contribution to the professional literature to any colleague I could trap in between classes.

Later, a letter came. It had a California return address. I knew instinctively who had sent it. Carl Rogers had read my article. He was now giving me his opinions. With nervous hands, I tremblingly opened the envelope and delicately unfolded the stationery within it. Sure enough it was from Rogers. However, instead of giving me new ideas, he gave me a piece of his mind. How could I compare him and his theory with Kohut and his object relations hypothesis? As Rogers pointed out, he had tested his ideas, and they were research-based. Kohut's thoughts were just that—thoughts! He had no empirical proof for his proposals.

I was surprised at the words from Rogers. They were stern. The unconditionally accepting man had drawn a line in the sand and basically told me not to cross it again. If I did, I knew I could be assured of at least another letter. At first, my feelings vacillated. I was sure that my opinions had merit. However, as I contemplated the epistle, I began to realize Carl Rogers had a reason for addressing me the way he did. He had given his life to building his theory, and the reputation of his person and his work depended on how what he had written was interpreted.

The two approaches I had focused on had entirely different research bases, and Rogers wanted to let me know his ideas had been empirically tested.

It was a teachable moment. Since then I have tried in my own work to be more careful in what I compare and how. I also read the literature with a bit more of a critical eye. Corrective feedback, even when blunt and unwelcome, can make a positive difference in the way we live and the way we look at research and theory.

chapter | 59

MY PAL SAL

When I became a counselor, I knew something about individual and group therapy but nothing about how to work with families. I assumed that I could use the skills I had refined with individuals and groups on families until I met my first family. Then I realized that reflection, "I" statements, and even confrontation were not the same when applied in such an environment.

Fortunately, within my counseling setting was a colleague who had received family therapy training at the Philadelphia Child Guidance Clinic. He offered to mentor and teach me how to work with families. However, he had one condition.

"Before I see a family with you," he stated simply, "I want you to read some books by Sal Minuchin."

Eager to make a good impression on him and to learn as much as I could, I said I would.

"But tell me," I said, "what has she written?"

My colleague looked at me in disbelief but said kindly, "'Sal' is an abbreviation for Salvador. I'll bring you a list of his texts tomorrow."

So I began my immersion into a field I have come to love. If my mentor had been overly sensitive or insulted by my ignorance, I would not have advanced in my knowledge. However, I was allowed to make mistakes and learn from them. Sometimes we, as counselors, need to remember that a mistake is not the worse thing that can happen to us or our clients. Such occasions provide educational opportunities.

chapter | 60

THUNDER AND POETRY

It had been a difficult day. My schedule had been jam-packed with a host of new clients who had some serious problems. To make it even more harried in the midst of the hurriedness, a series of storms had rolled through the area and played havoc with the electrical system. Therefore, there was turbulence both inside and outside my working environment. I wondered if my clients had been as disturbed by the disruptive atmosphere as I had. Rain was one thing; the chaos of a passing weather system was another.

I can still remember the bitter taste of almost cold coffee that I consumed twice that day with the hope that the dark liquid I poured from the pot would contain something hot. Both my taste buds and I had been disappointed. I can also still see the streak of lightning that grounded nearby and hear the crackle of an oak tree across the street that was split in two as a result of a direct hit. (I have actually wondered since if the violent storm so pivotal in the life of Martin Luther was of this nature. If so, I understand the non-*DSM-IV* term *conversion reactions* in new ways.)

Now it was late in the afternoon. Time for paperwork and the updating of charts. Time for reflection and attention to making sure I was documenting what I had done. The last session I had conducted had been particularly rough. The woman who was my client had been demanding. She wanted everything fixed now, and there was no reasoning with her. I could see why she was seeking treatment, but I thought after we finished working that I might need a good counselor too, if for nothing more than catharsis. After all, I was reading about primal scream therapy then. I could be a case of one, I thought, in a qualitative research experiment to see if such a release really was effective.

So I was glad for a break from the rush and fuss of the preceding events. However, as I was dutifully writing out clinical notes, a procedure that was routine and somewhat mundane, I found myself jotting down something different than usual. Instead of the prosaic, pathological, and intervention language I normally transcribed onto an 8 ½" by 11" yellow sheet of paper, I found poetic words were rhythmically flowing from my pen. It was almost as if they were demanding a life of their own outside the confines of my mind. I had the power to make their appearance possible and positive, or I could simply ignore them. I chose the former course because I must admit I was charged up already and excited to see where the process would go.

I had been working as a counselor for only a couple of years when this occurred, and this incident was not the first time I had had other than clinical words come to mind. However, this occasion was the first time I openly entertained the thoughts and emotions that accompanied poetic words. Thus, as the sunlight peaked through the clouds and played in the red and orange maple leaves outside my window, I wrote down the following sentences:

In the midst of a day that has brought mainly gray skies,
Hard rains, and two cups of lukewarm coffee
You come to me with Disney wishes
Wanting me to change into
A Houdini figure, with Daniel Boone's style,
Prince Charming's grace, and Abe Lincoln's wisdom,
Who with magic words, a special wand, frontier spirit, and perhaps a smile
Can cure all trouble in a flash.
But reality sits in a green cushioned chair, lightning has struck a nearby tree,
Yesterday ended another month, I'm uncomfortable sometimes in silence,
And unlike fantasy figures, I can't always be what you see in your mind.

To say that the writing of the words was transforming may be to overstate the case. However, I realized something fresh in the process of writing. I was calmer, and I had insight into my day and especially into the last session I had had. My graduate education had not prepared me for such an event, but then my professors had said counselor training was a lifelong event—not a sentence of two or three years. So, I thought, here is a lesson.

Counseling is an art as well as a science. We who are in the profession as practitioners, teachers, and supervisors need to pay attention to that artistic side of our discipline as well as the artistic side of ourselves if we are to be complete and competent. Unless we do, we will be mechanical and in the long run less than our best.

chapter | 61

WHO WANTS TO WORK?

When my son, Nate, was eight years old he informed me that he was learning the countries of South America just for the fun of it. After listening to him rattle off a few, I said, "Why not learn the countries of Africa?"

He replied, "There are too many. That wouldn't be fun; it'd be work."

Sometimes the number of factors that our clients face seems overwhelming. However, if we can help them clarify their visions, they are more likely to work toward realistic achievements. In the process, they are likely to become more connected with their friends, themselves, and their inner resources. They are also more likely to be productive in counseling. Some situations are simpler to deal with than others, like memorizing the names of countries in South America. Others require what Nate would describe as "African effort," that is, a focused dedication to the task at hand.

Regardless, I never ask clients in any setting what they want to talk about. Rather, I ask them what they want to work on. The emphasis of such phrasing may be subtle, but the outcome can be significant.

chapter | 62

THE PHONY PRISONER

I've lived in six different states during my lifetime. Moving, like aging, is not always a smooth or easy process. Saying "goodbyes" and "hellos" can be awkward as well as painful.

In the midst of the noise and activity that accompany such transitions, there is silence. The silence, if extended, can be disturbing and discouraging. I found this fact out when I moved from North Carolina to Connecticut. My new environment was full of potential and difficulties I never imagined. My residence was in a neighborhood where people valued their privacy. Thus, meeting my neighbors, let alone greeting or interacting with them regularly, was a nonevent; that is, it did not happen. My colleagues at work were professionally friendly, but none of them lived near me, and our relationships ended when the workday did. The small town where I lived did not have singles groups or other activity groups that I could gravitate toward. Thus, as time went on, I realized I was isolated. What a strange feeling. I was used to being social and actively involved in various projects.

"What do I do now?" was the reoccurring thought that crossed my mind. My situation is not going to change soon. As I thought, I continued to read. It was the time right after the Iranian hostage crisis. Then one day, as I put down the newspaper, I picked up my pen.

"Although I am not in the same dire straits as those Americans who were held hostage," I thought, "I am in a crisis that I do not have great control over. I can respond positively to life as Victor Frankl advocated, or I can get depressed. The former sounds better." Thereafter, for almost a year, I pretended I was a prisoner in my house and that I had control over only paper, a pen, and any ideas I could generate.

Thus, I ritualistically wrote each day as I reflected on what I had read in counseling and what was occurring in my own life. The results were several manuscripts that were later published as well as a habit I came to value. In 1999, I was cited as being in the top 1% of contributors to the *Journal of Counseling and Development* for the 15-year period from 1978 to 1993. Such a citation probably would not have happened had I not been in such dire straits and responded as I did. What we choose to do at any one time affects much of who we become.

chapter | 63

NOT BY WORK ALONE

Early in my career, I devoted almost all of my time to either counseling or writing about counseling. I was intense, and the payoff was publications. However, there was something missing. I realized the missing link when I went for an important job interview at a rather high-profile university as a counselor educator.

All went well until I had my interview with the dean of the school, who was pleasant but firm. He looked at my resume and in a rather serious tone said,

"I see you write a lot. There are a lot of publications here."

"Yes," I said (with a sense of pride). "I find it therapeutic."

Without missing a beat, he then said, "You must be very sick."

At the time I probably was sick, at lcast in a couple of ways. I was sick in the realization that this particular interview was virtually over and that the dean before me had recognized I was on the fast track to burnout because I was not doing anything outside the profession. I was also sick in that I was overfocused on my work instead of my overall life.

Just as we do not live by bread alone, living only to be a counselor or a writer may not be the healthiest thing to do. We need to think avocationally as well as vocationally. That means making time in our day for family and friends as well as fitness and fun. Since that interview I have taken the time to play games, relax at the pool, go on vacations, and talk more with my wife and children. It has been fun. I still write—a lot—but I enjoy it more and I control it rather than it controlling me.

chapter | 64

REJECTION

Few sentences in the English language are more frustrating to counselors who write than the words "Thank you for your submission, but we do not find it suitable for publication." The reason why the words are so emotionally devastating is because they are critical and counselors are sensitive. In addition, to be rejected is the antithesis of what counseling is about. Furthermore, a manuscript that is not accepted is work that many counselors look back on as effort that was in vain. They could have been doing something more productive, such as spending time with their family, relaxing with a hobby, or seeing clients. Therefore, they often become sad and despondent. However, I think the opposite reaction is called for. There is a challenge to rejection that calls us to inspect what we are doing, what we are saying, and the way we are conveying it to others.

I once had a manuscript that I thought had potential rejected by a periodical in which I thought readers would enjoy and benefit from reading it. I was downcast at first, but as I reflected on the critical comments, I could see that some were deserved. Therefore, in my spare time, I started cleaning up the manuscript. The next year, I noticed there had been a change in the editor of the journal to which I had submitted. Thus, I sent the revision back and waited. A few months later, a "fat" envelope with a rejection letter arrived in my mailbox again. I read the comments, put the materials away and thought. Then, I pulled them out again and once more started to revise. Three years later, the editor of the journal changed again. My manuscript was updated, revised, and resubmitted. The third time was the charm. The reviews were wonderful to read.

Rejection is not the worst thing that can happen to a paper or a person. Giving up is. Although unpleasant, rejection can lead to introspection and change.

chapter | 65

COUNSELORS ANONYMOUS

Development as a counselor continues after one's formal education has ended. There are seminars to attend on the latest trends in the field and continuing education experiences to participate in in order to hone clinical skills. Outside of these structured ways of professionally improving oneself, there are more informal means by which to grow, such as discussions with colleagues and even former students.

The never-ending nature of developing as a counselor was dramatically illustrated to me when I was a professor of counselor education at the University of Alabama at Birmingham. Some recent graduates invited me to join them after work at a local tavern to "talk" counseling. When I arrived, I found they wanted not only to engage in conversation but also to induct me into a group they had organized. The group was called "counselors anonymous" and was unlike any other "anonymous" organization that I have ever encountered. It was composed of practitioners who saw themselves evolving as the field of counseling grew. It was not that the individuals in the group were addicted to the profession. Rather, it was that they envisioned themselves becoming stronger and better as the profession of counseling increased in status and they improved their skills.

Thus, before this group I pledged to continue to strive to develop and to identify myself as one of them, that is, a counselor. There was no secret handshake. There were no papers to sign or membership forms to fill out. Rather, the only action I took that day was to continue to identify myself with the field of which I was already a part. I have by saying before every presentation I make: "My name is Sam, and I'm a counselor." I plan to keep doing this forever. Growing as a counselor is something from which I hope never to recover.

Points to ponder |

1. What has been your experience with supervision? How has it helped you grow?

2. When have you been rejected? How did it feel? What did you do (or wish you had done) to make the experience better?

3. Time is an important commodity. We sometimes take it for granted. In what ways do you use your time to grow personally and professionally? Are there ways you could use your time better?

Section | nine

DEVELOPMENTAL CONSIDERATIONS

When she turned 40
she took it hard
Like breaking an arm
or having a baby.
Awkward, painful, new,
she was hesitant in her moves
unsure of what to do.
Not knowing kept her going
without clear direction.
I met her at the crossroads.

Who we are and what we become as people and professionals are frequently tied in with how we face and react to events in our lives, especially the unexpected and unpredictable. Life is both funny and serious, and it is in seeing both sides, sometimes simultaneously, that we gain maturity that allows us to continue to develop.

The vignettes in this section are like those that have preceded them in that they are events as seen through the eyes of clients and a counselor that have made an impression on their lives. The senses of seeing, hearing, and touching particularly come to the forefront in these stories as they do in most incidents in life that we remember. As you read these pieces you may want to examine sensing times in your own life that helped make you more sensitive and alive.

chapter | 66

AGING BUT NOT DEVELOPING

Developmental crises demand our attention. Aging, having children, not reaching one's goals at a particular time, or failing to keep up professionally are examples of developmental events that can potentially create a crisis.

I once had a middle-aged woman come into my office who personified the power of stagnation. She was a graduate of what she described as one of the finest counseling programs in the nation. However, she had obtained her master's degree more than 25 years ago and had not opened a book on counseling since. Now she was inquiring as to what she could do with her education.

"Well," I said, "Are you nationally certified?"

She looked at me inquisitively and said, "What's that?"

"Well, certification comes through NBCC," I explained.

"I watch CBS and FOX," she countered.

"No," I replied. "NBCC is not a television station; it is the National Board for Certified Counselors."

"Oh?" she responded. "It wasn't around when I got my degree. I never heard of it."

So, I explained further. "Becoming a nationally certified counselor (NCC) might help you in getting licensed in this state because the test given is the same."

She looked puzzled and said, "I already have a license. I've been driving a long time, and as long as I keep my record clean, I won't have to take the test again."

"No," I said emphatically, realizing she was going to drive me crazy if I let her. "I'm talking about being licensed as a counselor in North Carolina."

"When did that happen?" she inquired in her Rip Van Winkle style.

"1983 was when the initial registration law was enacted," I said, "followed in 1994 with licensure."

"I wasn't that interested in counseling then," she replied.

"Well," I said, "Certification and licensure are important if you want to practice as a counselor. Likewise, becoming a member of Chi Sigma Iota would be good."

She seemed to beam at the mention of Chi Sigma Iota.

"I was their sweetheart in college," she said proudly.

"That is Sigma Chi," I countered. "This group does not have a sweetheart that I know of, although if they ever become interested in one, I'll let them know of your availability and experience. You should join because of their emphasis on excellence in counseling."

She smiled, but I could tell she did not give an iota about what I was saying regarding the counseling academic and professional honor society international. Thus, I changed the subject.

"Did you know in our department we have two CACREP-approved programs?" I asked.

Well, as soon as the words were out of my mouth, I wanted to retrieve them. She just stared at me like a deer facing the headlights of an oncoming car, shook her head from side to side, and whispered, "Does CACREP stand for what I think it does?"

And I said, "I don't think so. It is the Council for the Accreditation of Counseling and Related Educational Programs."

Well, the conversation continued going downhill from there. I did not dare bring up ERIC because I am sure if she heard ERIC moved from Michigan to North Carolina after growing up in Ann Arbor for 25 years, she would have made a comment about the restlessness of young adults. She also would have wanted to know who CASS was and why this couple did not have a last name because they apparently had an intimate relationship and had been very productive.

The point is that this graduate of a counseling program had not developed. Rather, she had mentally retired and was completely unaware of the changes and the language that had evolved since she last opened a counseling book. She was developmentally delayed in understanding where the field was, and whether she knew it or not, she was in a crisis because she was ill-informed.

chapter | 67

TREES WITH LIGHTS

I have a friend who took his three-year-old out to choose a Christmas tree. They went to a lot they had visited the year before, but the child did not remember the place or the personnel. Thus, the process of picking out a Christmas tree was new to the child. Therefore, my friend in a fatherly type of way started showing his son the trees from which to pick.

"Mike," he said, as he showed him a fine-looking and affordable tree, "Do you like this tree?"

The boy replied, "Yes."

"Do you want to buy it?" the father then inquired.

The young boy shook his head from side to side and answered, "No."

So they went to another tree, and the father asked again, "Mike, do you like this tree?"

The three-year-old again answered, "Yes."

"Do you want to buy it?" the father asked hopefully.

Again the same nonverbal response occurred, and the answer was "No."

This scenario went on for a few more trees until the father, somewhat frustrated and now less than filled with the holiday spirit, showed his young son one last tree. To the question of whether he liked the tree, the boy said "yes"; to the question of whether he wanted to buy the tree, the boy again replied "no."

In exasperation, my friend finally said to his son, "I don't understand. We have seen a lot of trees, and you say that you like them, but you don't want to buy any of them. Tell my why."

The young child looked down for a minute at the ground and then looked up at his father, and with the honesty and innocence of childhood he said,

"I was hoping we'd get a Christmas tree with lights."

The boy had not remembered that people put the lights on Christmas trees. All he recalled from age two was that Christmas trees had lights. In his mind, it made sense to get a tree that was decorated. He had a vision of what a Christmas tree should look like, but the vision was uninformed.

The same can be said for some of our clients who become excited after one of our counseling sessions. They have a vision of what their lives should be like. However, for the uninformed the path to achieving their vision is unclear. They do not realize that a dream becomes a reality only through hard work and over time. That is where our job begins.

chapter | 68

DON'T TAKE IT LITERALLY

Clients can be quite concrete. That is not necessarily bad, but there is a price to be paid if they are too concrete. In most cases it involves their talking about specifics that have nothing to do with their overall life. Even worse, actions can take place that are a bit bizarre. The latter happened to me once when I was working with a client who was back from the regional mental hospital. My task was to evaluate the client to see if he was ready to readjust to the outside world. However, no one instructed me how I was to complete this task. Instead, I was told, "You're smart. You'll figure it out."

Well, it was nice to think that others thought I was capable, but when the time came for the evaluation, I was still wondering what I was going to do. As I entered the waiting room, however, I got an idea by noticing the number of people in the room who were paging through magazines.

"That's it," I said to myself. "I will grab a few magazines. We will then look at the pictures together, and I will have my client tell me stories about himself related to the pictures."

So, I gathered some magazines, put them under my arm, and went back to the office with the client. We then started going through the pages after I gave him the following instructions:

"Clyde," I said, "We're going to look at some pictures in these magazines. I want you to tell me about what you see and how it relates to you."

"Okay" was his response.

The first picture was of a house. He related that he lived in one and that it was made of wood.

"Good," I said.

The second picture was of a forest. He said he liked the outdoors and being in the woods.

"Great," I stated.

The next picture was of a hamburger with fries, an advertisement for a national food chain.

"I'm hungry" was all he said, and with that he ripped out the picture and ate it.

"Feel better?" I inquired.

"Not really," he said. "It needed ketchup."

"Clyde," I replied, "I think you can get that and more back at the hospital. Let's go book you a room for a little while longer."

So we did, and Clyde gained the time he needed to get better.

chapter | 69

EROTIC OR ERRATIC: WHAT A DIFFERENCE A WORD MAKES

When I was stationed at Fort Lee, Virginia, as a part of my Army officer training for the Quartermaster Corps, I was assigned to a substance abuse unit. Because we were not always busy, I used to occasionally put on my tennis togs and go play tennis while many of my friends would play golf. Because of this difference in interest, I often went to the courts by myself. My hope was to get involved in a pickup game, and I am pleased to say that frequently happened. However, some times were better than others.

One of my more frustrating experiences came on a windy afternoon in April. I was playing next to another young lieutenant who was quite sincere but who was not very skilled. She kept hitting her tennis balls over to my court and, of course, kept running over to get them. I would like to report that she finally quit or that she improved, but neither occurred. I can report that she was polite. I tried to be well-mannered in return. However, I finally gave up my game when I realized how futile it was to keep playing under such circumstances.

Well, as fate would have it, a couple of weeks after this incident, I was at a party at the Officers' Club, where who should show up but this same young lieutenant. Seeing me, she waved and came over to where my friends and I were standing. Because she did not have a tennis ball or a tennis racket in her hands, I thought I had nothing to dodge, pick up, or be afraid of.

"I'm really glad to see you," she said. "You left so abruptly the other day. We didn't even have a chance to talk."

"Anyway," she continued, "I just wanted to tell you that I don't think I have ever been as erotic next to anyone in my life as I was with you recently on the tennis court. You were great to keep your sense of humor when I kept messing up. I promise next time I'll be better. I'm practicing."

"Excuse me?" I said.

"I was just too anxious that day," she explained. "If I hadn't been so erotic and broken your concentration, who knows what might have happened."

Well, her sentences kept rolling on, and she kept saying "erotic" for "erratic" until I was blushing pretty badly and my friends were thinking that a love set was more than I had described to them. Finally, I regained my composure and thanked her for her apology. Then I quickly exited her presence once more. However, since that experience I have realized the power of words anew and how different some words that sound similar are from others. I have also been more cognizant that counseling, like life, has its humorous as well as serious moments.

chapter | 70

LOST

When I lived on the coast of Connecticut, a friend from another region of the country came to visit. He flew into New York and rented a car. However, on his way to my house he got lost.

When the phone rang an hour past the time I expected him, I asked, "John, where are you?"

"I'm at K-Mart," he replied.

Stunned for a minute by his answer, I said, "John, Connecticut is bigger than it looks on the map. We have a lot of K-Marts here. Please give me another landmark so I can help you get to my house."

There was a pause on the line for a few seconds. The next thing I heard was "Fog-a-re-a. I'm in Fogarea."

Still confused I asked him to tell me more about "Fogarea." He then said, "I'm reading a sign. It says 'Fogarea for the next 10 miles.'"

"That's "'fog area,'" I said. "There's a lot of fog here by the water."

Clients sometimes find themselves in similar situations as my friend. They are in new territory. They get lost. One of our responsibilities as counselors is to help them get their bearings and then find direction. It seems so simple in principle, but the process itself is fraught with potential miscues and confusion.

chapter | 71

RESILIENCY AND UNPREDICTABILITY

People are resilient and sometimes solve problems in creative but unpredictable ways. I have found this out with clients and even with members of my own family. Let me illustrate.

Some years ago, my then-preschool second child, Nathaniel, was interested in playing what he described as a "real" game of baseball with me. I tried to dissuade him and just play pitch, but he insisted, even up to the point of calling balls and strikes. Thus, the game began.

I pitched the first ball, and Nathaniel swung, missing by a wide margin. "Strike one," I announced.

I pitched again with the same results. "Strike two, Nathaniel," I said.

Looking more determined than ever, Nathaniel stepped up to the piece of wood serving as home plate in our front yard. Then I pitched again—a high, slow, floating ball that could have had a sign on it reading "hit me, I'm easy"—but alas Nathaniel swung and came up empty a third time.

"Strike three," I yelled. "Nathaniel, you are out."

Nathaniel dropped his bat, hung his head, and slowly started walking away from home plate. I wanted to rescue him and yell, "It's okay. Come back," but I just watched. As I watched I imagined joining the local chapter of "bad parents anonymous." However, Nathaniel suddenly turned around with a smile on his face, marched confidently back to home plate, picked up the plastic bat he was using, and said,

"Dad, I'm a new person."

Sometimes our clients gain a new perspective on an otherwise dismal situation in surprising ways and act accordingly. Being an effective counselor is giving oneself permission to wait for an action as well as to act on a feeling. In such moments, a metamorphosis may occur, and a new person may emerge.

chapter | 72

FINDING A VISION THAT WORKS

It was a minor crisis that, like most crises, started small. I walked quietly into the kitchen one summer morning without making a sound. There was Claire, my wife, looking at a can of tomato soup that she had placed on a counter. Not only was she gazing at the can, but she seemed to be doing a simple dance as well. She would take a step forward every few seconds and then a step back. As opposed to a "fox trot," she was doing what I would later describe as a "soup step." However, it was her focus on the soup, not her movement, that caught my attention the most.

"Hmmm," I thought. "Either she likes this tomato soup can and is planning on surprising me with a tangy new breakfast entrée or she is having trouble with her eyes and is trying to find the right spot from which to read the soup's label."

So I asked innocently, "Honey, what are you doing with that can of tomato soup?"

"Nothing," she replied. "I am just checking out the best spot in this kitchen to stand so I can read the soup's contents clearly."

Thus, I knew instantly that any dreams I had of seeing my wife serve a new item on our limited breakfast menu were just that—fantasies. Likewise, I breathed a sigh of relief that we would not be going to the Fred Astaire dance studio soon. On the other hand, I knew that the reality of Claire going to see an eye doctor was fairly dim, too. After all, our house had a lot of counters from which cans can be viewed. However, after talking together about the situation, an appointment was made for her to see an optometrist at, of all places, one called VisionWorks. That visit corrected my wife's eye problem, and she began to have even more close encounters with tomato soup cans, packaged food stuffs, and people.

After a crisis should come a vision, just like after a storm should come a rainbow. If we, as counselors, are going to be helpful and healing, we need to assist our clients in creating realistic and fulfilling visions and goals. We should encourage them when needed to correct their vision in order to read the fine print as well as to see the big picture. We should do likewise for our own mental health and well-being. Life is good, but to get beyond crises, one needs a focus—a vision if you will—that goes far beyond kitchen countertops.

Points to ponder |

1. How have you developed personally and professionally in the past few years? Whom do you know who is stuck developmentally, and how do you see yourself and others interacting with that person?

2. What has been your experience in getting lost? How did you feel? What was most helpful to you at such times?

3. Resilience is an important quality in life. When have you seen it displayed in others or yourself? What kind of a difference did it make?

Section | ten

TERMINATION

Death caught my father by surprise.
He had other activities planned for that April day
like weeding the garden and listening to a Braves' game.
Yet startled as he was
he had the presence of mind
to empty his pockets
before the ambulance came.
I am sure he did not know that he had suffered a triple aneurysm
(I doubt he would have cared).
My father was accepting
he loved plants and people, especially his family,
he was aware of his own mortality.
In sadness
I find relief
(and even comfort)
in knowing how well he lived.

The end of an event is usually not the climax of the experience. Yet, termination is important in counseling because it offers closure. Too often termination is minimized or neglected. The result is that learning that has occurred prior to the end of the counseling experience may be lost. In this section, "The Quilt" illustrates how a proper ending can have a profound impact on a client. "Hair" goes beyond focusing just on the client to show how we as counselors are affected by the end of life and relationships. "On Grief and Gratitude" deals with personal loss also and how we respond when death is "within the family." This section ends with a little humor and the optimism of Gordon Allport in "Always Becoming."

chapter | 73

THE QUILT

I once worked with an elderly woman. She had had a terrible life and was destitute and distraught. She was also dying. The facts of her life were pretty plain and straightforward, but she had not been able to come to terms with her situation or get relief from the troubles that had surrounded her. In the midst of a rather depressing session, I asked an unusual question because the obvious ones were not working.

"So what do you do for fun?"

"Fun" was not a theme running through this woman's life, and to introduce it seemed a bit bizarre, but after looking at me with rather sobering eyes, she said, "I sew."

"I don't," I replied, "but I know that sewing is an art, and I've always admired people who could do it. Would you bring some of your sewing into the sessions?"

She agreed to, and the next time we met she did just that, spending most of the session telling me about her work. I then asked if she was still actively engaged in sewing. "Yes," she responded. As we talked, she came up with an idea of sewing a square patch of cloth that represented something important in her life that she wanted to resolve. From then on she came in with patches that represented different aspects of her life, many of which were adverse, such as the death of one of her children, her divorce, the loss of her energy as she grew older, and the pain of poverty. There were a few positive patches that she brought in also, like the memory of a special friend from adolescence and a trip she had once made to New York City.

One day she came without a patch but with a brown paper grocery bag. I kidded her that she must have sewn all night. In all seriousness, she replied that she had. Then she reached into the sack and brought out a small patchwork quilt. It contained all of her pain and the few bright spots in her life. It was not elegant, but it was beautiful. At the top, she had embroidered the word "PEACE" in blue thread on a white background.

"I'm at peace," she said. "I can now face life or death with serenity."

A few months later she died. I was saddened by her passing, but I knew she had left her bitterness behind. Through her art of sewing, she had made connections in her life that allowed her to grow and accept herself as well as find some meaning in her existence.

chapter | 74

HAIR

As a graduate student I went to New York and saw the Broadway play "Hair." But that's not what this story is all about. Instead, it involves a young woman I worked with in counseling. She was gaunt when I first saw her dressed in an oversized white tee shirt, blue jeans, and tennis shoes. However, her bony features and baggy clothes did not take me back nearly as much as the fact that she was bald. I am sure my face must have given away my surprise, for she said immediately on meeting me,

"My hair fell out last Tuesday. Radiation treatments will do that to you."

"I don't normally see women without their hair," I said. "I must admit the sight of you has caught me off guard. You have cancer?"

"Yes. It's in the early stages, and I intend to beat it. But I need some help. I need an ally."

Thus, we began with an explanation and admission on her part and an acknowledgment and inquiry on mine. We worked that summer and into three more seasons. Hair became the least of my concerns. Her strength and ability to function dominated my thoughts when I was with her.

I would love to say that she won the battle for her life and that her hair came back. Neither happened. However, from our sessions I learned a lot about courage and grace. I watched her fade but not without a fight that was heroic.

To this day, whenever I look at a young woman with flowing thick hair I think of that client. I realize that it is beneath such a rich exterior that the essence of a person lies. Hair sometimes hides the beauty of a person or tragically prevents it from developing.

chapter | 75

ON GRIEF AND GRATITUDE

It occurred unexpectedly. The voice mail message was from the veterinarian. "Eli has had a stroke and is struggling. He is not responding to treatment. I may have to put him to sleep. Please call me." I looked at my watch. It was 6:15 p.m., and the clinic had closed for the day. I was in Florida, 600 miles away from North Carolina. I had no choice but to wait until the following morning to find out the fate of my 16-year-old dog. Thus, heavy-hearted I walked back to my motel. I knew the night would be long and the outcome would most likely be what I feared the most.

Eli had come into my life when I was in my early 30s. He was a blessing. As I moved through the ranks of academic circles and up and down the east coast, Eli was my steady companion and confidant. He accepted Claire, my wife, and each of our three children as they entered his life. He was open to change and adaptable to new experiences. Even in old age he appeared to enjoy our family and always took his naps near us. Now he was struggling for his life, and I was helpless to help him.

The next day I called the vet as early as possible, and the doctor informed me of Eli's death. My heart sank, my throat grew thick, and my eyes welled up with water. I tried to speak, but my voice kept cracking, and there were long pauses in between words. "We'll save his body for you" were the final words of the conversation. So when I arrived back in Winston-Salem, I went to pick up Eli for his last ride home. That afternoon, with care, I buried him next to the backyard fence he had loved to patrol. Each child and Claire said good-bye to the dog that had shared his life with us. The funeral was bittersweet, filled with fond memories and deep sorrow.

Pets and people come into our lives in many ways. The experiences we have with them often make us more sensitive and open to the world. In death, there is a sadness but also a celebration. We become more aware of who we are in relationships as memories mingle with tears. Letting go of that which was and those we love is difficult. Saying hello to emptiness, the unknown, and new beginnings is painful. Amidst it all and above it all, however, we can be grateful. Even in loss there is life. It is the life of having been. Such a realization gives us hope for the future. If there have been good old days, there may be good new days as well. As the late Dag Hammarskjold (1965) said in his book, *Markings,* "For what has been, 'thanks.' For what will be, 'yes.'"

chapter | 76

ALWAYS BECOMING

The phrase "always becoming" is attributed to Gordon Allport. He believed people were continuously developing, and so do I. Even at termination there is growth, although we and the clients with whom we work do not always see it clearly.

In my quest to become a counselor, it took me many years of study to obtain the necessary degrees. The process became so long that when friends would ask my father what I was going to be when I finished, he would quip,

"He's going to be old!"

Actually, my father knew, as did I, that the termination of study would lead to a graduation and to a new life and lifestyle.

We, as counselors, often have difficulty with endings. Beginnings and renewing are much more enjoyable. However, every exit is also an entrance. So as you finish this book be aware that experiences turned into memories make a difference. New chapters in life begin when old ones come to a close.

Points to ponder |

1. Recall and write down important milestones and memories in your life. What have you done to resolve those situations that were difficult transitions for you? What are some ways you could come to terms with them?

2. Think of positive traits that you have admired in someone who has died. How could you incorporate some of these qualities into your own life?

3. What do you want your legacy to be as a person? As a counselor? Write a paragraph about what you would want others to say about you.

Epilogue

Finishing a book that is both personal and professional in nature, like this one, can produce a plethora of thoughts and emotions. For example, you may feel validated or energized as well as disappointed that the end of the text was reached too soon or that certain situations were not covered. I have similar thoughts and feelings. Such bittersweet responses are natural and to be expected.

My hope is that some of the stories you have read in these pages will influence you positively and help you be a bit different than before. Furthermore, it is also my wish that you will carry some of the stories forward into your life and that they may enrich and delight you as a part of your memory. Finally, I hope that you will see counseling as a profession that is filled with a great variety of experiences where your skills, insights, and creativity will be tested in ways that will spark both your growth and that of your clients. If any of these three experiences happens, then your completion of these pages may lead to new beginnings, including the writing and telling of your own stories as a counselor. Who could ask for more?

Notes

[1] From *Reality Sits in a Green Cushioned Chair* (p. 17), by S. T. Gladding, 1976, Atlanta, GA: Collegiate Press. Copyright 1976 by S. T. Gladding. Reprinted with permission.

[2] From "Patchwork," by S. T. Gladding, 1974, *Personnel and Guidance Journal, 53,* p. 39. Copyright 1974 by the American Counseling Association. Reprinted with permission.

[3] From *Group Work: A Counseling Specialty* (3rd ed., p. 196), by S. T. Gladding, 1999, Upper Saddle River, NJ: Prentice Hall. Copyright 1999 by S. T. Gladding. Reprinted with permission.

[4] From *Family Therapy: History, Theory and Practice* (2nd ed., p. 199), by S. T. Gladding, 1998, Upper Saddle River, NJ: Prentice Hall. Copyright 1998 by S. T. Gladding. Reprinted with permission.

[5] From *Group Work: A Counseling Specialty* (3rd ed., p. 44), by S. T. Gladding, 1999, Upper Saddle River, NJ: Prentice Hall. Copyright 1999 by S. T. Gladding. Reprinted with permission.

[6] From "Reflections on a Professional Friendship," by S. T. Gladding, 1989, *Journal of Humanistic Education and Development, 27,* pp. 190–191. Copyright 1989 by the American Counseling Association. Reprinted with permission.

References

Gladding, S. T. (1974). Patchwork. *Personnel and Guidance Journal, 53,* 39.

Gladding, S. T. (1976). *Reality sits in a green cushioned chair.* Atlanta, GA: Collegiate Press.

Gladding, S. T. (1989). Reflections on a professional friendship. *Journal of Humanistic Education and Development, 27,* 190–191.

Gladding, S. T. (1998a). *Counseling as an art: The creative arts in counseling* (2nd ed.). Alexandria, VA: American Counseling Association.

Gladding, S. T. (1998b). *Family therapy: History, theory and practice* (2nd ed.). Upper Saddle River, NJ: Prentice Hall.

Gladding, S. T. (1999). *Group Work: A counseling specialty* (3rd ed.). Upper Saddle River, NJ: Prentice Hall.

Gladding, S. T. (2000). *Counseling: A comprehensive profession* (4th ed.). Upper Saddle River, NJ: Prentice Hall.

Gladding, S. T. (2001). *The counseling dictionary.* Upper Saddle River, NJ: Prentice Hall.

Gladding, S. T. (2002). *Family therapy: History, theory and practice* (3rd ed.). Upper Saddle River, NJ: Prentice Hall.

Hammarskjold, D. (1965). *Markings.* New York: Knopf.

Lerner, A. (1978). *Poetry as therapy.* New York: Pergamon.